Number One

A Play

Jean Anouilh

A SAMUEL FRENCH ACTING EDITION

SAMUELFRENCH-LONDON.CO.UK
SAMUELFRENCH.COM

Copyright © 1985 by Jean Anouilh and Michael Frayn
All Rights Reserved

NUMBER ONE is fully protected under the copyright laws of the British Commonwealth, including Canada, the United States of America, and all other countries of the Copyright Union. All rights, including professional and amateur stage productions, recitation, lecturing, public reading, motion picture, radio broadcasting, television and the rights of translation into foreign languages are strictly reserved.

ISBN 978-0-573-01619-6

www.samuelfrench-london.co.uk

www.samuelfrench.com

FOR AMATEUR PRODUCTION ENQUIRIES

**UNITED KINGDOM AND WORLD
EXCLUDING NORTH AMERICA**
plays@SamuelFrench-London.co.uk
020 7255 4302/01

Each title is subject to availability from Samuel French,
depending upon country of performance.

CAUTION: Professional and amateur producers are hereby warned that *NUMBER ONE* is subject to a licensing fee. Publication of this play does not imply availability for performance. Both amateurs and professionals considering a production are strongly advised to apply to the appropriate agent before starting rehearsals, advertising, or booking a theatre. A licensing fee must be paid whether the title is presented for charity or gain and whether or not admission is charged.

The professional rights in this play are controlled by United Agents LLP, 12-26 Lexington Street, London, W1F OLE.

No one shall make any changes in this title for the purpose of production. No part of this book may be reproduced, stored in a retrieval system, or transmitted in any form, by any means, now known or yet to be invented, including mechanical, electronic, photocopying, recording, videotaping, or otherwise, without the prior written permission of the publisher. No one shall upload this title, or part of this title, to any social media websites.

The right of Jean Anouilh to be identified as author of this work has been asserted by him in accordance with Section 77 of the Copyright, Designs and Patents Act 1988

NUMBER ONE

The original French text of the play, entitled *Le Nombril* (The Navel), is published by La Table Ronde, 40, rue du Bac, Paris VIIe.

Le Nombril was first presented in Paris at the Théâtre de l'Atelier on the 24th September 1981. It was directed by Jean Anouilh and Roland Pietri, with Bernard Blier as Léon.

Number One — a somewhat condensed and adapted version of the original — was first presented at the Theatre Royal, Windsor (in association with H.M. Tennent Ltd) on the 13th March 1984, and transferred to the Queen's Theatre, Shaftesbury Avenue, London, where it opened on the 24th April 1984. The cast was as follows:

Léon Saint-Pé	Leo McKern
Housekeeper	Ruby Head
Joséphine, Léon's girl-friend	Linda Jean Barry
Arthur, his son	John Michie
Doctor	Anthony Sharp
Gaston, his friend	Joe Melia
Lucie, his daughter	Shirley Cassedy
Ardèle, his wife	Margaret Whiting
Bernard, his son-in-law	Peter Blythe
Marie-Christine, his daughter	Ceri Jackson

Directed by Robert Chetwyn
Designed by Sue Plummer

The action of the play takes place in Léon's studio in the attic of his house

ACT I*

A huge attic studio in an old house

Enter Léon, an ageing playwright. He has a monstrously bandaged gout, like someone in a seventeenth-century play. But he hobbles gamely across to his desk to start the day's work, talking to himself to keep his spirits up

Léon Enter Léon, an ageing playwright. He has a monstrously bandaged gout, like someone in a seventeenth-century play. But he hobbles gamely across to his desk to start the day's work, talking to himself to keep his spirits up. (*He sits down*) He sits down. And at once inspiration comes to him.

Enter the Housekeeper

Or rather the housekeeper comes to him.

Housekeeper There's a leak in the bathroom. The wall's completely sodden and next door's going to be complaining again, not to mention downstairs, because if it goes on like this they're going to have it pissing down. We'll have to get the plumber back. We ought to have one living in. Be a bit simpler with an old barn like this.

Léon makes a gesture of resignation

And your son phoned. He said he was going to look in some time this morning about some trouble he's got.

Léon makes another gesture of resignation

The Housekeeper exits

Léon hobbles across the room

Léon (*muttering*) So tiresome having only one foot. Though one could get by if the rest of the world would only leave one in peace.

Enter Joséphine. She is an attractive woman, attractively dressed, between twenty-five and thirty—much younger than him, at any rate

Joséphine I'm going out.
Léon Right.
Joséphine Aren't you going to ask me where I'm going?
Léon No.
Joséphine (*tears coming to her eyes*) Then I won't go. (*She sits down, piqued*) Never cared what happens to me, have you?
Léon (*making a polite effort*) Yes, I have. I do. Of course I do. Where were you going?
Joséphine (*getting up, irritated*) Mind your own business!

Léon makes another gesture of resignation

---
*N.B. Paragraph 3 on p ii of this Acting Edition regarding photocopying and video-recording should be carefully read.

(*From the doorway*) I'm going to an audition, if you must know. They're looking for someone to play Joan of Arc. I haven't read the script, I just know it's my sort of part. There are sixty-nine of us being auditioned, and sixty-eight of us will have a letter of recommendation. I shan't have one. I'm the girl-friend of a playwright and not a soul in the business do I know.
Léon Perhaps that will make you stand out from the crowd.

Joséphine makes a contemptuous gesture and goes out, slamming the door

Léon makes another gesture of resignation. He hobbles back to his chair and picks up the decanter of whisky, singing to himself

> He said, "I've only one leg
> So I've got to have a peg..."

He has a sudden twinge in his foot, and grimaces with pain. He sits down

(*Growling*) It's miserable enough being ill, without having to stay teetotal on top of it! (*He takes his packet of cigarettes out of his pocket puts one in his mouth, then after due consideration puts it back in the packet*) No. That's banned as well. Do you want cancer? The charlatan! Bursting with health himself—and he thinks he can treat others! What an egotist!

Enter the Housekeeper with the post

(*Barking*) Now what is it? I'm working.
Housekeeper The post.

She puts down the letters and goes out

Léon (*growling*) More tediousness. Correspondence course is it now. (*He sorts throught the letters mistrustfully*) Careful now. Watch out for the long ones— they've always got bills in. Here we go—a letter from Gaston. (*He opens it and reads*) "Léon, my dear old friend. I've got terrible problems and you've absolutely got to help me. Remember when we were in short trousers..." (*He puts the letter back on the pile. Growling*) If only the letter were the same length as the trousers. (*He opens another letter with sudden eagerness*) Aha! Black edges! Another Redskin bites the dust! (*He reads it and murmurs dreamily*) Fifty-eight. So young! Well, youth's a stuff will not endure. (*He finishes, and puts the funeral announcement on the pile*) I feel particularly well this morning. I'll bury the lot of them. Only one fly in the ointment—it would have been nice to do it while I was still young enough to enjoy it. (*His gout suddenly pains him*) Agh! (*He groans*) But why me, a man who has shunned all excess? Apparently it skips a generation and you end up paying for your grandfather's fun. I sometimes wonder what he can have got up to, the old devil, to land me with this lot. Maxim's every night, and nothing but the best. And the bill? Oh, that's for afterwards, that's for the grandson to pay! Bastard! Egotist! Bourgeois swine! And then you're surprised if everyone turns socialist!

Act I

Enter his son Arthur. He is about thirty, with boyish good looks. He is being tragic, and overdoing it slightly

Arthur Hello, Papa. Papa, I rang your housekeeper first thing because I've absolutely got to see you.
Léon (*haughtily*) All right. Take a good long look at me in silence, and then hop it. I'm working.
Arthur (*exclaiming, wounded*) Papa! I'm your only son!
Léon So you've been telling me for the last twenty-seven years. You do go on about it, you know. It's becoming obscene.
Arthur Papa, this time it's serious.
Léon (*coldly*) Everything is always serious. There's only one thing to do, and that's to act as if it weren't. Then it all settles down. Events can get discouraged, too.
Arthur Very well. (*Tragically*) It will be all your doing!

Arthur exits

Léon (*left alone, growling*) All *my* doing? What have *I* done? Heaven blessed our union with issue, that's all, and it's a blessing that goes on and on. I wonder heaven hasn't got cramp in the arm by now, it's blessed away for so long. (*He sighs bitterly*) It's like kittens; very sweet while they're still kittens. But when kittens grow up you give them to the neighbours. They go and claw up the carpets in somebody else's house.

The telephone rings. He picks up the receiver, listens, and replies in an assumed Asiatic voice

He no here. He go out. (*He hangs up*) Nothing to it. Properly trained staff, that's all you need. (*He settles himself resolutely at his desk*) To work! What at, though? "That is the question", as they say in England. (*He reflects gloomily for a moment, then woefully concludes*) Now there was a good play. Unfortunately it wasn't by me. As is generally known. The muses flee me like so many girls. As age creeps on I must be starting to smell. (*He absent-mindedly lights a cigarette*) Perhaps because I smoke too much? Oh, damn it! Three puffs and that's it! (*He takes three puffs and stubs the cigarette out*) That's worse! It was the fourth puff that was going to be the good one ... (*He bursts out furiously*) Oh, they've made a lovely job of it! Once upon a time you died in peace. It was a sticky moment, and you got through it as best you could, with the help of religion. Now we all die the same way—without benèfit of clergy, but with tubes all over the place instead, and getting the wind up about it ten years too soon. That's medical progress for you! (*He adds, after some reflection*) Though of course it's all covered by insurance. (*He makes a decision*) To work! That's the only thing that does you any good. In theory it ought to make up for the lost joys of tobacco. I say "in theory" because in fact it's working that makes you want to smoke. (*He bursts out*) Oh, damn it, I'll have one! (*He takes it out of the packet and then puts it back*) No, I won't have one. (*He writes a word*) That's a good title. *Les Misérables.* There's the novel by Victor Hugo, of course, but the dictionary belongs to everyone, genius or no. *Les Misérables.* I'll stick with it. (*He broods for a moment*) And what indeed I should like to write is a play about egocentrics. The unhappiest creatures on earth, as everyone knows. It stands to reason; they never meet anyone except other egotists—because everyone's an egotist, after all—so they live in a state of permanent frustration. How could people possibly be concerned with themselves, and not with *them*? They can't understand! They're outraged! People may be egotistical—all right—but not as egotistical as *that*! (*He broods for a moment*) But how to get all this across without explaining it? That is the question! As they keep saying in England. Oh, damn it—I'll just have a quick one ... (*He lights a cigarette*)

Enter the Housekeeper

Housekeeper It's the doctor.

Léon hurriedly puts his cigarette out

Léon Hell's teeth! Nearly got caught! It reeks of smoke in here, too! I'm for it! (*He fans the air round him with his pad of paper*)

Enter the Doctor, carrying his bag and overcoat

Doctor! How are you this morning? Not looking too good, I see.

The Doctor stops in surprise

Doctor Really?
Léon (*leading him away*) I'll open the window for a moment. A little fresh air will do you good.
Doctor (*uneasily*) It'll be cold, though ...
Léon (*opening the window wide*) Not at all. Very mild out. Indian summer.
Doctor (*struck by the remark*) What makes you say I'm not looking well?
Léon You seem drawn. And rather pale. Are you always as white as that?
Doctor (*glancing in a nearby mirror*) It's all those stairs up here. Fancy not living in a modern block!
Léon In the eighteenth century this *was* a modern block!
Doctor (*setting up his sphygmomanometer*) Supposing I made you install a lift, on doctor's orders? Pull up your sleeve. Anyway, gout or no gout, you'll have to go and see Abject about your heart. I'm going to insist on that.
Léon Who's Abject?
Doctor He's the top heart specialist in Paris. Costs the earth now he's fashionable, the old so-and-so, but he's the top man.

He has been taking Léon's pulse as he talks. Léon has taken his wrist as well

Good. Pulse seems to be all right.
Léon (*still holding his wrist*) How about you? Have *you* seen Abject recently?

Act I

Doctor (*his eye on his watch*) Had dinner with him the day before yesterday. Why?
Léon (*solicitously*) Because *your* pulse isn't all right.
Doctor What are you doing, fiddling around with me. Anyway, how could you have taken my pulse? You haven't even got a watch!
Léon I was looking at yours.
Doctor (*operating his sphygmomanometer and laughing*) And what was my pulse, in the opinion of my esteemed colleague?
Léon (*coldly*) A hundred and twenty.
Doctor (*with a start*) You're joking!
Léon (*gravely*) I never joke with a patient. Check!
Doctor Good God! You're right!
Léon (*solicitously*) There are my stairs, of course. But they don't usually do that to you ...
Doctor (*puzzled, taking his pulse again*) No, they don't.
Léon Don't panic. It may be just some passing thing. Go home. Use your lift. Put your feet up, and ask Abject if he can come and have a look at you.
Doctor (*pumping up his sphygmomanometer, a little anxious in spite of himself*) Very funny. He's at hospital in the morning, and you can't disturb a big man like him, even if you're a personal friend, just because your pulse is racing a little. Hardly a matter of life and death.
Léon But it may very easily be the symptom of something that is.
Doctor (*recovering his firmness, as he puts his instrument away*) Enough of this foolery. Do you know what your blood pressure is?
Léon No, but I have the feeling you're just about to tell me.
Doctor (*coldly*) One hundred and seventy over one hundred.
Léon (*blenching in his turn*) Is that high?
Doctor (*icily*) Yes.
Léon (*groaning; indignantly*) But last week I was only one hundred and sixty over ninety—and you told me *that* was high!
Doctor (*jovially, rather sadistically*) Yes, because it *was* high!
Léon (*suddenly very angry*) So that's how you do your job, is it, you total incompetent? You vulture! Can't wait to get me into hospital, can you, with tubes all over the place, bound hand and foot, defenceless and ridiculous—while you swan around in your lovely butcher's overalls, showing off your bulging biceps to your harem of love-sick nurses? You sadist! What's your blood pressure, anyway? Get your coat off! I'm going to take your blood pressure for you!
Doctor What?
Léon Get your coat off!
Doctor (*yelping furiously and struggling*) Take your hands off me at once! I'm the doctor, not you!
Léon We'll see! I'll fix you up with a three hundred over two hundred— that'll scare *you* to death, you bastard!
Doctor (*managing to disengage himself and recover his apparatus*) This is a disgusting display! You seem to forget that I'm a leading doctor!
Léon Yes, and I'm a leading patient! And, patient or impatient, I'm a

great deal stronger than you! (*He seizes the Doctor in an armlock*) Right, then. A little pressure, and bang goes your ulna. So what's your diagnosis, Doctor?
Doctor (*yelping, his body twisted*) Stop! You're hurting me! Let me go, it might break! It's very fragile! (*He bawls*) Help!
Léon (*holding him*) You're wasting your breath. There's no one here apart from my housekeeper, who is utterly devoted to me. It's still feudal in this house! You socialist! (*He feels in the Doctor's bag with his free hand, without letting go of him*) Anyway, I'm going to give you an injection! That'll buck you up a bit! (*He throws various things aside and finds what he is looking for*) Disposable syringes. That's a bit of luck when you've only got one hand. (*He searches*) What shall we give him a shot of? We'll take one at random!
Doctor (*his body twisted, terrified*) No! No! Not just anything! You're mad! Some of them are poisonous! Not an injection, I beg of you! (*He groans piteously*) A pill instead!
Léon A pill? Why?
Doctor (*piteously*) I'm terribly scared of injections.
Léon (*firmly, but slightly mortified*) Come on, now! A big boy like you!
Doctor (*defeated*) I can't do it. I was in the Resistance—twice decorated—personally congratulated by de Gaulle—but I'm terribly scared of injections.

Léon releases him, mollified, and gives him a hearty clap on the shoulder

Léon Ah! A human remark at last. I have a feeling we might become friends ... Sit down for a bit then, Doctor. It's not good for your heart, all that kind of thing. A little whisky, perhaps, as a pick-me-up? A harmless cigarette?
Doctor (*defeated but unbending*) I never drink alcohol and I don't smoke. And may I remind you that you are categorically forbidden to do either?
Léon (*lighting a cigarette*) I know, but I've really earned this one. (*He offers his arm obligingly*) All right. Take my blood pressure again. And try not to doctor the figures this time.
Doctor (*complying; furiously*) Very well. The only reason I'm doing it is because I've taken the Hippocratic Oath—but after that display of violence you're going to have one hell of a reading, I can promise you that!

He pumps furiously away. He gazes at the dial in disbelief. He starts again, sombrely watched by Léon, who is a little uneasy in spite of himself. Finally he admits with vexation

One hundred and fifty over eighty.
Léon (*exclaiming in delight*) You see? A little exercise has done me good!
Doctor (*stunned*) I don't understand it. I simply don't understand it!
Léon There at last speaks a true scientist. (*He examines him in a more kindly light*) How nice it is when a doctor admits that nature is beyond him.
Doctor (*furiously*) It's incomprehensible! You were one hundred and sev-

Act I

enty over one hundred not five minutes ago! (*He anxiously takes his own pulse*) And I'm still one hundred and twenty.

Léon (*kindly*) That's because I've relaxed in the meantime, and you haven't.

The Doctor shakily finds his overcoat and puts it on

You obviously find it difficult to relax. Look at you! You've never consulted any of your colleagues on the psychiatric side?

Doctor (*with a smile*) No, but then I'm not the one who's ill; I'm the doctor.

Léon The two things aren't mutually exclusive. Do you dream a lot?

Doctor (*sharply*) Regularly.

Léon Could you tell me your last dream?

Doctor Of course. What for, though?

Léon (*woodenly*) It's something that concerns me as well. My life is in your hands. We ought to get to know each other a little. It's not much to ask...

Doctor (*smoothly*) Why not, then? If it helps to set your mind at rest... The whole essence of medicine is a relationship of trust between doctor and patient... You can tell me yours afterwards... Last night I dreamed that I was at my parents' house in the country, a place they must have sold ages ago... Night was falling. it was very dark... Mama had given me a terrible telling-off, and I'd turned into a little tiny garden flower that she wouldn't water. So then along came Caius, our great St Bernard. He towered over me like some mythological beast... He came closer... (*He hesitates for a moment, and then adds blushingly*) And he lifted his leg over me.

Léon (*imperturbably*) And that made you feel better?

Doctor (*as red as a lobster*) Yes. (*In some embarrassment he smiles at nothing in particular*)

Léon (*neutrally*) Well, we all have our problems. It's high time doctors realized that you have to attack the source—the problems themselves. The researchers are wasting their time making life hell for rats and monkeys—that's never going to tell them why men die.

Doctor (*primly*) My dear sir, medicine has made enormous strides!

Léon Descriptive strides, linguistic strides... You've found scientifically precise names for all the different ways of dying. But you haven't found why people die, when they're made to last a hundred years... (*Suddenly he shouts*) I want to know why I die! And I want to know right now! This is an emergency! Or else I'll put another armlock on you! (*He sets upon him*) Hup! We twist the forearm, and all at last becomes clear to the tortured doctor! You can't break the lock—so where's the key? The key to the whole damn enigma? The key, the key or I break your arm!

Doctor (*defeated, his face contorted with hatred*) You think you can stop what's coming to you by taking it out on me?

Léon No, but it keeps me going. I've got a simple mind. Wretched as we are, we can still laugh. (*He suddenly releases the Doctor and gets out his packet of cigarettes*) A quick smoke, Doctor, to get your breath back?

Doctor (*furiously, rubbing his arm*) No!
Léon You're making a mistake. You're depriving yourself of a great pleasure. And pleasure is another thing that's important for your health. It's just that we've spent the last two thousand years being afraid of it. (*All of a sudden he asks mockingly*) Supposing it was a man's soul that broke so easily, Doctor?

Black-out

The Lights come up again at once

On stage—Léon, sitting at his desk, still wearing his dressing gown, and with his foot still heavily bandaged, smoking a cigarette. Gaston, a good-looking, stylish man in his fifties, is walking tensely back and forth in front of him

Gaston You plainly never think about anyone but youself!
Léon (*woodenly*) Put yourself in my place. If I didn't who would?
Gaston You've never thought about anyone else since you were so high! Some people turn into egotists as they grow older, but you took to it in infancy. You had a gift for it. In primary school already—because may I point out that when we first met we were in blue check pinafores and short trousers. You'd perhaps forgotten that?
Léon (*coldly*) Impossible. You remind me of it every time you're on the borrow.
Gaston Because for me there are some things that are sacred ... I mean, I'm no saint. I've often been an absolute bastard, like everyone else. I've deceived my wives, I've betrayed my friends—just like everyone does. I let my old mother die alone because I had a dinner-party that night and I didn't want to miss it'... (*He gives a woebegone sigh*) But there is one thing that has always remained intact deep down inside me, and that is our childhood friendship. It was my little nest-egg of decency. You know? The one bit of capital you never touch! Many's the time I've said to myself, in front of my shaving mirror in the morning: "Gaston, you are beneath contempt". And then I've thought yet again about all the things I did for you when you were a little boy—and I've forgiven myself.
Léon (*coldly*) You're too kind-hearted.
Gaston Yes ... When you come right down to it I'm too kind-hearted. Many's the time you've given me cause for complaint. The occasions when you let me down are beyond number. At first I held it against you, but then I said to myself: "No, Gaston, he's your friend. When you first knew him in the playground at primary school ..."
Léon (*finishing for him*) He was wearing a blue check pinafore and short trousers.
Gaston Exactly. So then I'd forgive you for what you'd just done to me as an adult. The nest-egg, you see! The bit of capital you never touch!
Léon The bit you can always borrow against.
Gaston (*struck by this*) It's funny, you know. You're an artist, but all you can talk about is money.
Léon Possibly because that's all anyone ever talks to me about.

Act I

Gaston Naturally, the royalties you get. Then there's the film rights, foreign rights ... Lot of money there—no point denying it, I'm not the tax man.
Léon And all these rights and royalties, you think, impose certain responsibilities on me?
Gaston In a way. You can't have rights without responsibilities. That's the ABC of ethics. Your plays are very commercial and my novels are very demanding.
Léon You mean, they don't sell?
Gaston What's fifty thousand francs to you?
Léon Old francs?
Gaston New francs.
Léon (*coldly*) It's fifty thousand francs.
Gaston How can you be so sordid? You're not going to tell me you'd lose much sleep over fifty thousand francs? I'm drowning. Your old childhood friend is drowning. And it's not because I've lost at poker this time, it's not because I need a new car. (Though incidentally I do need one—mine's always breaking down—the repairs are ruining me) It's for a highly moral purpose; it's to get married with. To someone who's the love of my life.
Léon Another one?
Gaston (*rather sheepishly*) All right, I've been married four times before. But anyone can make a mistake, you know.
Léon Not as often as that.
Gaston What can I do—I'm hounded by fate! It's a little indelicate of you to draw attention to it. You're a sadist at heart. You love holding my head under water. You get a real kick out of it, don't you.
Léon I could have done without it this morning. Your perpetual drowning gurgles are making me waste precious time. I can only work in the morning, and I can only work while I'm smoking. That's been banned by the doctor, and you've already made me waste a cigarette listening to you. (*He stubs his cigarette out*) This one was killing me for nothing.
Gaston (*lighting one*) You're banned from smoking, are you? Doesn't worry you if I smoke, does it? I'm so tense. I only keep going on pills. Two to get me to sleep at night; two to wake me up in the morning; two to give me an appetite for lunch; two to digest it; two to get my weight down—because with the pills for giving me an appetite I'm eating too much; and two to build me up, because the slimming pills run me down ... We've got ways of treating things now, thank God!
Léon And you know which pills are which, do you?
Gaston Of course. They're different colours. (*He takes a tube out of his pocket and swallows a couple of pills*)
Léon What were those for?
Gaston They were extra. They were for calming me down when I get too tense. You could have spared me those two! All you had to do was to say yes.
Léon (*stonily*) But the answer's no. I'm sorry. Take another two.
Gaston (*sourly*) Our friendship isn't worth fifty thousand francs?

Léon No.
Gaston (*pathetically, after a slight pause*) Thirty thousand. I'll cut down on the reception. I won't ask anyone except the witnesses. I'm giving you a discount for old times' sake.
Léon No.
Gaston (*rising, icily*) Very well. It will be all your doing.

Gaston exits

Léon (*exploding as soon as he is alone*) All my doing? What will be all my doing, for heaven's sake? Unless it's getting myself a little peace from them all. Enough's enough! I owe myself to my work. Here we go. *Les Misérables.* A play in two acts. (*He writes the words and then gazes at them*) All right. *Les Misérables.* What next, though? Ay, there's the rub. Oh, damn it, I'll have one! (*He takes a cigarette and then puts it back in the packet*) No, I won't have one.

Enter the Housekeeper

Housekeeper It's the plumber.
Léon Again? What now?
Housekeeper He says he can't mend the leak. He says all the plumbing's got to be changed. He says wait another six months and all the bathroom fittings'll have to be changed, too!

Léon makes a gesture of resignation

Exit the Housekeeper

The telephone rings. Léon replies in an assumed voice

Léon He no here.... No, no, I no he. I he live-in foreign couple. (*He hangs up*) They're getting suspicious. Life will become unliveable. It's impossible to concentrate. Oh, damn it, I'll just have one.

Enter Lucie like a whirlwind, followed by the Housekeeper. Lucie is in hat and gloves, and has come from outdoors

Lucie Papa!
Housekeeper It's Madame Lucie.
Lucie Papa, this is too much!

Exit the Housekeeper

Léon (*calmly*) What's too much?
Lucie Your utter selfishness.
Léon (*putting down his pen resignedly*) What have I done now?
Lucie Nothing. That's the trouble. Not a thing from when I first asked you to help. Bernard is an absolute washout, for all his airs and graces. I've been telling you so for years and you do absolutely nothing whatsoever to protect me. I am your daughter, after all.
Léon (*gently*) My dear girl, you never asked me for my opinion when you got married. I'd have given it to you there and then.

Act I

Lucie (*shrugging*) There and then I shouldn't have believed you. Have you never been a woman in love?
Léon (*naïvely*) No. Perforce not.
Lucie It's easy to sit in judgment when you've a stone where your heart should be. Anyway, life with that man is no longer liveable.
Léon He's deceiving you?
Lucie Certainly not. I'm deceiving him. There comes a time when a woman has the right to live her own life, doesn't there? He pretends not to notice, simply so as to humiliate me. Just like a man—he always has to have the best part to play. You know what he's like—he never thinks of anyone but himself! I want a divorce.
Léon Oh, Lucie...
Lucie I do have my self-respect.
Léon (*gently*) You've also got two children...
Lucie (*barking*) Blackmail, of course! Just as I expected. When will people stop going on at women about their having children?
Léon When they stop having them. It will come with progress.
Lucie (*calmly, rather absurdly*) My womb belongs to me!
Léon Certainly. But through a quirk of nature it was their home for nine months. And they're not likely to forget the fact.
Lucie (*shrugging and lighting a cigarette*) What a conformist you are, when you think of the rackety life you've led!
Léon (*growling*) The rackety life I've led? I've spent my life being a father. In the end I shall turn out to have held more babies in my arms than women. Up and down the bedroom in the middle of the night, in pyjama top and bare backside, when you so long to sleep, you'd like to howl yourself.
Lucie (*suddenly hard*) When you and Mama separated I was twelve. That's a detail you seem to forget. (*She stubs out her cigarette*)
Léon (*becoming sombre*) I know. And I have a lot of trouble forgetting it. Life had become unbearable. Everlasting reproaches and sobbings over her disappointed ambitions, over nothing. I'd come to a complete standstill. I couldn't pay the bills!
Lucie So you passed them on to us. I'm not talking about Marie-Christine, who'd already gone off with her first young man. It was Arthur and I who paid the bills. We were the ones who cried—going off to school, coming back in the evening, when it was time for home-work. And we were supposed to do well at school on top of it all! Are you surprised if Arthur at the age of twenty-seven is a mere playboy who has never done anything with his life? That's your handiwork. Oh, it's wonderful to see you moralizing away with your marvellously pure heroines. It may fool the audience—but it doesn't fool us. (*She tensely lights another cigarette*) Please note that I'm not reproaching you.
Léon (*sombrely*) Of course not. I realize that.
Lucie We're not still living in the Middle Ages. The individual is perfectly free. People must be allowed to live their own lives. (*She inhales tensely*) So you're not allowed to smoke now?
Léon (*gloomily, fiddling with his packet of cigarettes*) No.

Lucie (*smoking*) I'm on two packs a day. No way I can cut down in the state I'm in. Does it worry you if I smoke?
Léon No. It reminds me of the good old days, when I was a chain-smoker. (*With sudden simple truth*) I'm old, my dear, I'm ill, and I've got to the time of life when the accounts have all been cast. There are no reproaches, even, left to be made. I have bowed to them all already.
Lucie (*bitterly, with a derisive laugh*) Of course. Now you're going to start using the state of your health to make us all feel sorry for you. It will be your last bit of theatre.
Léon I hope not.
Lucie (*casually*) Are you writing anything at the moment?
Léon I'm trying to. When I manage to get a little peace. It's a play about people who never think of anything except themselves.
Lucie (*going back immediately to her theme*) There was nothing left between Bernard and me, and I have the right to be a woman. With Roméro I have at last achieved plenitude.
Léon (*repeating the word gloomily*) Plenitude. What a lovely word. For all one's pretensions to culture there are some words one forgets. It means you make love better with this one, does it?
Lucie (*up in arms, blazing*) Have you no respect for anything?
Léon (*gently*) Oh, yes. A great many things. I sometimes find it an embarrassment. Still, let's confine ourselves to plenitude. You want to get a divorce and marry him?
Lucie (*stubbing out her cigarette*) Oh, no! I'm going to be very sure of myself, I can tell you, before I do anything as stupid as that again.
Léon You mean you're not sure of yourself?
Lucie (*lighting another cigarette*) Look, I've only known him for three months.
Léon I see. A trial offer of plenitude. And what precisely are you expecting me to do?
Lucie To speak to Bernard. He's got tremendous respect for you, like all the rest of them who saw your plays when they were very young. He'll take it if it comes from you.
Léon And do I have to explain to him about plenitude?
Lucie Up to you. You handle it however you like. That's your end of the business. I leave the choice of argument to you.
Léon What about the children? Are you leaving the choice of children to Bernard?
Lucie (*crying angrily*) Certainly not! I'm their mother, and I'm keeping them.
Léon Are you sure you couldn't do this little job for yourself? You're a big girl now. I'm a little out of my depth with all this plenitude.
Lucie No. Because there are all the financial questions to be settled—how much maintenance he'll have to pay me. You'll be able to talk about all that so much better than me. Anyway, you know what Bernard is like. If I told him he might get all huffy and tragical about it and see himself as the wronged husband. Roméro and I are off to Fontainebleau for the weekend, and when I come back I'm going to find it's all been settled,

Act I

without any pointless dramas. You can be terribly persuasive when you want to be!

Léon (*timidly*) How about the children? Am I the one who has to tell them?

Lucie Oh, don't worry about the children. At their age they think everything's tremendous fun! They'll have two fathers instead of one. They'll be thrilled! Bye bye, then, sweet kind lovely Papa. I'm relying on you to rescue your poor daughter! Next Monday, as soon as I get back from Fontainebleau, I'll come round and you can tell me all about it.

She is about to go out when he suddenly calls her back

Léon Lucie!

She turns round

I loved you so much when you were little. I thought I was the one you took after. Your mother was preoccupied with her endless grievances, so she wasn't exactly overflowing with milk and honey, and your brother was a little beast ... But when it came to you, I couldn't help feeling ...

He doesn't finish; she cuts him short

Lucie Yes, but you left me all the same. (*She adds brightly*) Anyway, water under the bridge, Papa.

She goes out

Left to himself, Léon meditates rather sadly for a moment, then suddenly cries

Léon Oh, damn it, I'll have one! (*He lights a cigarette and begins to hobble around the empty armchair, addressing it as he goes*) My poor dear Bernard ... No. Sounds melancholy. If I'm too sorry for him he's going to start crying ... My dear old Bernard ... No. A little too familiar, given the circumstances ... Bernard ...! No. Too bald. (*He makes a fresh start*) Dear Bernard ... (*He stops*)

Gaston has come silently in, and is standing stiffly in front of him

Gaston All right. Twenty thousand. I won't buy her an engagement ring. It'll be a shabby little saving, but I'll tell her the reason.

Léon looks at him in silence, then writes a cheque

Léon Here. We're a pair of cowards.

Gaston (*pocketing the cheque after a quick glance to examine it*) You despise me, don't you. You've always despised me. My friendship has had to be rock-solid to weather your contempt! You know, I sometimes feel sorry for you. Do you think we can go through life without ever caring about others? Do you think you're alone in this world?

Léon (*rather naïvely*) I've come to the conclusion I'm not.

Gaston (*exclaiming*) Oh, that irony of yours! That coldness, that fearful coldness! There are days when that coldness of yours makes me want to just sit down and cry like a baby! (*He suddenly bursts out sobbing*)
Léon (*limply*) Come on, now ... Be sensible ... Don't get in such a state about it ... I did give you your cheque, after all ...
Gaston (*bitterly, through his tears*) Half. Not even half. I can't go on! The pity of it—the disillusion—I just can't bear it any more! I can see the two of us now—ten years old, in the school playground, with our little blue check overalls ...
Léon And our short trousers—I know. Come on, pull yourself together. That was a long, long time ago, and we've grown up now.
Gaston Friendship's never meant much to you, has it.
Léon On the contrary—it's meant a great deal to me. In fact I've believed more in friendship than in love. Love always has a lot of small print at the bottom.
Gaston (*struck by this*) You really are hopelessly cynical! What have you got in there where your heart should be?
Léon That's a question I've often been asked. A muscle, I suppose, like everyone else. And now this muscle turns out to be tired. It doesn't pump properly any more, and that makes my temper a little uncertain.
Gaston (*groaning*) What about me? Don't you think I'm ill, with all the pills I take? I'm going to have to take a couple more, damn it. It's all your fault. I'm beside myself with worry. (*He swallows his pills*) Absolutely beside myself.
Léon (*gazing at him half amused and half saddened*) Is it nice out there?
Gaston (*failing to understand*) Out where?
Léon Beside yourself. One has so few chances to get out and about.
Gaston (*taking a moment to understand, then his attitude suddenly hardens*) What about you, then? You think you're not an egotist?
Léon Yes, I'm an egotist. But I'm a subtle egotist; I've spent my life looking after others— for my own personal advantage, I'm sure. It must be so nice to believe one's in love.
Gaston (*pathetically, rather ridiculously*) It's wonderful, believe me! Not that one's sufferings are over. Take me—always in love, heart as full as a sponge—I'm in perpetual agony. So is Clothilde, I can tell you.
Léon Clothilde? Who's Clothilde?
Gaston My fifth wife ... Or soon will be, thanks to you ... She's had such an unhappy life! She's been married four times, as well. And her childhood! If she told you about her childhood you'd weep, you'd sit down and weep! Oh yes—it takes courage to bind yourself, for ever and ever, amen, to someone so broken by life!
Léon (*calmly*) You'll get used to it. In the first place, nothing lasts for ever and ever, amen. You've already demonstrated that four times over. And secondly, we always have courage enough to bear the misfortunes of others.
Gaston (*impressed*) Is that one of yours?
Léon No, it's one of La Rochefoucauld's, but I've always been sorry it wasn't one of mine.

Gaston (*venomously*) You know what a deeply embittered man he was, your friend La Rochefoucauld?
Léon There are so many like him with less talent than he had.
Gaston (*bitterly, after a moment's pause*) Is that a dig at me? You don't like my work, do you?
Léon I do ... I do ... I don't always understand it, but I'm full of admiration.
Gaston (*offhandedly*) Well, there are a lot of things in this life that go over your head. I've got used to it. I take you as you are. My friendship goes deeper than that. In years to come people are going to be amazed at my friendship with you. But I shall just laugh in their faces. I'll tell them "There's one thing you know nothing about," I'll say, "and that's friendship! He was a shade facile, certainly ... But he was my friend! We first met in primary school ..."
Léon (*absent-mindedly, as he looks at the papers on his desk*) In short trousers and blue check pinafores.
Gaston (*irritated*) I see. If I'm disturbing you why don't you say so? You're not only an appalling egotist—you're a hypocrite as well!
Léon To tell you the truth, when you arrived I was just about to start a new play.
Gaston (*amused and superior*) And what's it going to be called, this new masterpiece of yours?
Léon *Les Misérables.*
Gaston You know that's a novel by Victor Hugo?
Léon How very kind of you to warn me.
Gaston (*lightly*) Well, happy hunting! Oh, these men of the theatre! Just let the pen rip and away they go! No need to think—all you've got to do is chatter chatter chatter. (*He hesitates for a moment on the threshold*) You haven't had second thoughts about the engagement ring? It would have been a nice gesture. Something of the warmth of our childhood friendship that I've told Clothilde so much about.

Léon flaps his hand

All right. I won't go on about it. You'll only end up by making me feel humiliated.

Gaston exits

Léon *Les Misérables.* No. First the other thing. (*He broods for a moment, and then begins sententiously*) My dear Bernard ...

Black-out

The Lights come up on the same

Leon is still in his dressing gown, with his stick, and with his foot still heavily bandaged

Sitting stiffly around him are: his wife Ardèle; Lucie and her husband Bernard; and his other daughter Marie-Christine. His son Arthur is also present, in sombre mood, walking tensely up and down at the back of the room

Léon (*facetiously*) So, this is what you might call a family council?
Ardèle (*primly*) Call it whatever you like. The children told me what was going on, so in view of the seriousness of the situation I decided to come here, where I had sworn I would never set foot. Is that woman out of the house?
Léon (*imperturbably*) That woman is out of the house.
Ardèle Out, and who knows where? The whole of Paris is laughing at you, my dear!
Léon (*flapping his hand*) Paris has got to have its fun. It's the fun capital of the world.
Ardèle If you want to be made a fool of—well that's your business. You play at being a young man and you're a grandfather, poor dear! When those little angels say, "Where's Grandpops? Why do we never see Grandpops?"—what am I supposed to tell them?
Léon (*secretly irritated*) Tell them not to say "Grandpops". Tell them it's stupid and vulgar.
Ardèle (*giving a derisive and mirthless laugh which is rather like the whinnying of a horse*) He he he he!
Léon (*mimicking her angrily*) What's that supposed to mean—he he he he!
Ardèle It means I'm laughing.
Léon Then laugh. Don't whinny.
Ardèle (*turning to the others, blazing with anger*) You hear the way he treats me? A man I have given my life to! You're all my witnesses? It's all very well for his children—they've had to put up with it for years—and after all he is their father—they have to bear their cross just as I do. But in front of Bernard! In front of a poor boy who thought when he married Lucie that he was coming into a respectable and united family! I'm sorry, Bernard! I blush for you. I blush for your family, for the Montmachous who did us the honour of allying themselves with us. Poor Bernard! Poor boy! He's come down to earth with a bump.
Léon (*annoyed*) Not with all that big a bump. Leave Bernard out of it. Firstly because he's always known about our separation, secondly because I don't suppose he gives a damn, and thirdly because he's very shortly going to have other reasons for coming down to earth with a bump. A much bigger bump.

Lucie, who has made herself very small, merely gives an anxious cry

Lucie Papa!
Ardèle (*frostily*) What do you mean by that?
Léon Nothing.
Bernard (*stiffly*) I must tell you, Father-in-law, that although I have made it a rule not to become involved in any of the differences you and Mother-in-law may have, this is a matter on which I share her views entirely. The family is sacred; children are sacred; and nothing—ever—on any pretext—must be allowed to threaten this stability. This is the view taken by my wife—who is of course of irreproachable character herself—and it is also the view that I take——

Act I

Léon (*interrupting*) My poor dear Bernard...!
Lucie (*brightly*) Papa! I'm not going away for the weekend until Saturday.

Léon stops, and takes a cigarette out of his packet

Léon Oh, yes. Right. Goodness, this is all too complicated for me. I'm going to have one.

Ardèle gives an aggressively derisive laugh

Ardèle You're forbidden to smoke!
Léon Yes. There are very few things I'm allowed to do.
Ardèle (*sourly*) Up to you, of course, if you want to gamble with your health.
Léon Let's get down to business. Why have you all come marching round here in a body this morning?
Ardèle To put you on your guard.
Léon Against what?
Ardèle Against that whore. Because she's making use of your senile passion to try and fleece you, you poor booby.
Léon Aha! Now we've got there! Who's been telling you this?
Ardèle Madame Lemoine.
Léon Madame Lemoine. And who is Madame Lemoine?
Ardèle My clairvoyant. She looked in her ball and saw someone trying to get you to sign something. Her ball is quite categoric. Someone is trying to cozen money out of you.
Léon You don't need second sight to divine that.
Ardèle A woman. Young. Not family. There's no doubt about it. So you still believe a man of your age might be loved for himself alone, do you, you poor fool. Forgive me if I laugh! He he he he!
Léon (*howling in exasperation*) For the last time, I beg you not to whinny, or I shan't be responsible for my actions!
Ardèle (*to the others*) Now he's threatening me! He'll resort to violence. And it won't be for the first time, either! I've had grounds for divorce twenty times over! I've only desisted because of your family, Bernard.
Bernard Thank you, Mother-in-law. In our family, it has to be said, we don't divorce. I'll go further—I'm sorry if I'm treading on any toes here, Father-in-law—but we never put ourselves in a position which could give grounds for divorce. Never!
Léon (*his temper rising*) My dear Bernard, I have never put my nose into your family's affairs, but if you're going to take that tone, then allow me to inform you—
Lucie (*brightly*) Papa! You know I'm not going away until Saturday?
Léon (*finishing more calmly*) Then allow me to inform you that my daughter is not going away until Saturday.
Bernard (*uncomprehending*) I know. I don't see the connection, though.
Léon No connection at all. It's merely something we must all try to keep in mind.
Bernard I don't follow you.

Léon (*retreating*) Don't attempt to follow me—it wouldn't get you anywhere. I'm saying the first thing that comes into my head.
Ardèle (*with a disparaging laugh*) As usual! As witness your last few plays, poor dear. No wonder you're not a success any more. You're not the man you were. The marrow's being sucked out of your bones. You're being used up. When you were with me you were still writing tragedies.
Léon Understandably.
Ardèle If you hadn't left me you might have got the Nobel. You can say goodbye to that now. They know the whole story over there in Sweden. And they don't fool around when it comes to morals!
Léon He he he he! You make me feel like whinnying!
Ardèle (*to the others*) He's going too far. You're all my witnesses to that! He'll have no peace until I'm dead—or until he is.
Léon (*growling*) You fire first, then, I insist.
Ardèle Anyway, I shall be the perfect widow. That I vow. You'll never have to suffer any unfaithfulness on my part—not even when you're dead. I shall respect your memory. You can carry that certainty into your grave with you.
Léon Oh, that's bucked me up no end! I feel better already. I'm almost cured. (*He walks cheerfully about the room, then suddenly stops with a roar of pain*) Agh!
Ardèle Now what?
Léon My foot. It can't have heard.
Ardèle (*sourly*) Do stop clowning around—you're not on the stage! Are you or are you not, as Madame Lemoine says, in the process of arranging for a large income to be paid out of your estate to the creature you live with? It's not myself I'm thinking of. No-one can touch the houses you bought in my name. You thought you were cheating the tax man, didn't you, my dear, and all the time you were cheating yourself! But what about your rightful heirs, the children of your loins—are you going to let them be robbed? She's a schemer, that whore, she's a wolf in sheep's clothing. She's had no success in the theatre despite everything you've done for her—making a complete fool of yourself in the process for all Paris to see—so now she's started playing at nurses. And you're such a soft touch, that just for once—off stage, of course—she's in danger of having a success.
Léon (*stonily*) This seems indeed to be a serious matter, and one that certainly justifies this mass migration. The corpse will consider his defence. (*He looks at them all. Facetiously*) Whatever else, though, it's brought me the pleasure of seeing you all assembled. Families are so scattered these days! Marie-Christine, it's ages since I last saw you. How is Alonzo?
Marie-Christine (*primly*) I don't know, and I've no particular desire to know.
Léon I'm sorry! I'd only got as far as the South American decorator. What nationality is your current gentleman?
Marie-Christine Tony's English. We're getting married next month, as soon as his divorce comes through.

Léon I went so far as to have a morning suit made for your first wedding. It still fits me. Shall you invite me?
Marie-Christine (*flatly*) No, I shan't. It's going to be a strictly private wedding.
Léon Oh. I'm sorry.
Marie-Christine And while we're on the subject you and I must have a serious talk. Tony earns a perfectly good living—he's a photographer on *Paris-Match*. But I can't expect him to support me, you realize.
Léon Why not, if he's marrying you?
Marie-Christine Marriage has changed since your day! It's a partnership now, where everything is strictly shared. Wives work these days.
Léon (*exclaiming*) Ah! A bit of good news at last! You're working?
Marie-Christine You know perfectly well I'm not. I haven't found anything that suits me. But there's no reason why Tony should have to foot the bill just because he's marrying me.
Léon Rest assured, your allowance will remain the same.
Marie-Christine (*bitterly*) The same! When will you bring yourself up to date, Papa? You know you can't live even halfway decently on what you've been giving me ... Even less so when there are two of you.
Léon (*imperturbably*) It's quite true—I don't know what we're coming to. Life gets harder and harder. The price of cashmere goes up from one day to the next. (*He turns to Arthur*) How about you? What are you up to?
Arthur (*sombrely*) You wouldn't listen to me this morning when I tried to tell you. I've got the bailiffs in.
Léon Give them my regards. They're old friends of mine. (*He turns to Bernard*) My dear Bernard, we haven't much in common, and to be quite frank I've always found you rather heavy going. But you will never know how grateful I am to you for one thing: you've always managed to earn a living and support your family, in true Montmachou style. In this family these traditions are less firmly established. I shall miss you.
Bernard (*haughtily*) Miss me? Why?
Lucie (*crying out*) Yes, why?
Léon (*flatly*) If you had an accident. So deadly, the weekends, so deadly dull.
Bernard Your little witticisms are dismal. They haven't made anyone laugh for a long time.
Lucie They're also in the worst possible taste.
Léon You too? I'm obviously going to be the only soul in Paris they still get a laugh from.
Ardèle You know your father prides himself on never taking anyone seriously. Labour as he might to raise the tone of his plays, they've remained irredeemably popular. Even in the most heartbreaking circumstances, the best he can do is a contrived spoonerism. Brecht, Ionesco, Beckett—they've all taken the human condition seriously! But not him! (*She sighs*) I've not been a happy woman in this life!
Léon (*rather thoughtlessly, as he gets a twinge*) Neither have I.
Ardèle Let's get back to the matter in hand. What are you reckoning to leave to that whore when you're gone?

Léon (*lightly*) A few memories, I trust.
Ardèle (*whinnying*) He he he he! Can you see her—in black, with a little bunch of violets in her hand, communing on your grave! On her back, more likely, straight off! With a nice fat income by way of loving memories, and with the first long-haired lout to come down the street! In black! I'd like to see her! In any case I'm the one who'll be your widow! No-one else! And I'll forbid her the cemetery!
Léon (*his temper rising*) I shall get her a pass!
Ardèle With you dead it won't be valid! When will you stop saying the first thing that comes into your head!
Léon When things have some meaning to them. As a child, I got into the way of thinking that things had some meaning—and that's what I never recovered from.
Ardèle (*shrugging*) Don't put on your poor beaten cur act. We're not in the theatre and there's no-one to feel sorry for you here ... That thoroughly banal idea has been the subject of most of your plays, and you've wearied your family to death with it, poor dear ... If only you'd come out openly for permanent revolution, like Sartre, and cultivated the Absurd! But not you. You haven't even made the effort to be obscure! If only for the sake of your family! It wasn't much to ask! With a little will to work you could have been avant-garde, like everybody else ... Look at your friend Gaston ...
Léon (*suddenly howling*) Oh no!
Ardèle (*ironically*) What do you mean, "Oh, no"? Are you jealous of him? Can you deny that he has whole articles devoted to him in the intellectual press?
Léon Avant-garde? Oh, he's avant-garde all right! He's just about to get married for the fifth time! And to celebrate the occasion he came and touched me for fifty thousand francs!
Ardèle (*with a start*) Old francs?
Léon New francs.

The family is cast into gloom. Ardèle gives a roar of horror

Ardèle (*calling upon the others to witness*) Oh! You see where your father's money goes? And when he's so cheeseparing with us!
Léon (*rather sheepishly*) I took the coward's way out and compounded for twenty thousand. He got me by the short trousers again. He accused me of never thinking of anyone but myself.
Ardèle (*yelping*) What about us? Didn't you tell him that your first thought had to be for us?
Léon No. It had gone out of my head for a moment.
Ardèle You see what sort of man you are? You never think of anyone but yourself!
Léon (*pathetically*) That's what he said.
Ardèle (*carrying right on, calling upon the others to witness*) Twenty thousand francs for that talentless layabout, that phoney leftist! While my car won't go half the time! I've heard of cowardice, I've heard of egocentricity, but this is ridiculous! (*She adds bitterly*) I would have made

do with a little Mini, since we're reduced to penury ... And there's the twenty thousand francs for the car gone.

Arthur (*shouting, his face scarlet with rage*) I'm sorry, Mama, but there are some things in life that are more urgent than getting a new car! I've got the bailiffs in! And if I don't keep a proper standard of living for Christina I'm afraid she's going to leave me ... I can feel how fed up she is at the hard time we're having. We couldn't go skiing this winter, and she's absolutely nothing to wear!

Ardèle (*beside herself*) You can tell her, if it's any consolation, that my mink is worn bald! You've never managed to do anything with your own two hands, my poor boy, for all the education we gave you. You couldn't so much as screw a bulb into a socket! All you can do is screw money out of your father! And as for that model girl you saw fit to marry—all she needs to do to earn the housekeeping is to go back to the rag trade. They'll put clothes on her back. Women work these days!

Arthur (*barking*) You work, do you?

Ardèle (*with thunderous dignity*) I am your mother! I brought you up, while your father was hanging round actresses' dressing-rooms. I run my house! With one solitary maid! An illiterate Spaniard who can't even cook an egg in French. I live like a pauper so that your model girl can go out every evening and wriggle her scrawny behind in café society!

Arthur (*leaping up*) Mama! I'm not having anything said against Christina! She's worth more than you and your daughters put together!

Marie-Christine (*with a derisive laugh*) That tart?

Arthur (*turning on her, blazing*) That tart, as you call her, has been faithful to me for four whole years! How many times have you changed horses in that time—and always at Papa's expense?

Marie-Christine (*yelping*) I got married every time!

Arthur What difference does that make? You can still be a tart with the mayor's blessing. Can't you, Lucie!

Marie-Christine (*giving a great bellow, and throwing herself sobbing into Ardèle's arms*) Mama! He called me a tart!

Ardèle You've no right to go insulting your sisters, you rotten little cad! If your father were a man you'd get your face slapped for that. Here! (*She slaps his face*)

Bernard (*springing on Arthur*) Not my wife, anyway, who is someone of irreproachable character! And don't you forget it, you ill-mannered lout! (*He slaps Arthur's face*)

Arthur (*slapping Bernard's face back*) Are you looking for a fight, you rotten little shit? I'd go and pick one with your chum Roméro, if I were you!

Bernard With Roméro? Why Roméro?

Arthur Ask my sister—she'll tell you why.

Lucie (*hurling herself upon Arthur and slapping his face*) Oh! You little swine!

Arthur (*slapping her back*) You bastard!

Léon, who has remained impassive, rings the bell on his desk

Léon Calm down. Half-time. Let's not make a great drama of it. I have the distinct impression that it's merely a question of money yet again. (*He gets out his cheque-book*) What do you need to get rid of the bailiffs?
Arthur Twenty thousand.
Léon Old francs?
Arthur New francs.
Léon (*writing the cheque, and as he does so asking Ardèle*) What about you, for your poverty-stricken little Mini?
Ardèle (*primly*) Twenty thousand. I'll pay the rest out of my meagre allowance.
Léon (*writing the cheque, asking Marie-Christine*) And what about you, so you can marry your photographer without its costing him anything?
Marie-Christine Twenty thousand.
Léon (*writing the final cheque*) The set lunch for everyone. So no-one's going to feel hard done by. (*He turns to Lucie*) You're not after money, are you?
Lucie (*demurely*) No, Papa.
Léon "No, papa." Thanks to Bernard. Oh, but I'm going to miss the Montmachous!
Bernard Why?
Léon For no reason at all. There we are, then. It wasn't cheap, but I hope I have purchased my peace and quiet. The doctor has banned all emotion, any kind of shouting or commotion or trouble. They're just as bad as alcohol or tobacco. I could have a heart attack at any time.

Gaston suddenly bursts in looking tragic and pale

The warring family regroups at the sight of him

Gaston (*panting*) I absolutely must see you at once ... I'm interrupting. I'm sorry, you've got your family with you ... You've got to help me, it's desperate!
Léon What?
Gaston (*tragically*) It's Clothilde. She was terribly hurt you wouldn't buy her a ring. ... She's in a state of nervous collapse. She's packed her bag. If we don't do something at once she'll go back to the gutter where I found her. Talk to her, I implore you! Persuade her! For the sake of our boyhood friendship, open your heart for this once! We had blue check pinafores ...
Léon (*finishing for him*) And short trousers, yes, I know. Where is she?
Gaston Downstairs, sobbing her heart out in my car. Which has broken down, just to crown it all. I'll have to turn *that* in for a new one, as well!
Léon Right, then.

He starts to go out, and collides with the Housekeeper as she enters

Housekeeper It's the plumber. He says he can't mend the leak and he says you'll have to have all the pipes in the building changed. He says it's going to take six weeks at least, with all the water turned off, and he

Act I

says it'd be better to move out for the duration. And your lady friend's come back and she wants to know if she can go into her room and use the toilet, because the plumbers have broken the one in the hall while they were mending it, and she says family or no family she needs to have a wee.

Léon (*imperturbably*) Right. Let's all keep very calm. We'll try to get the whole thing sorted out.

The Housekeeper exits

Bernard (*pronouncing stiffly*) My dear Lucie, what a set your family are! No wonder your mother's a broken woman now...

Ardèle, transformed, very much the woman of the world, advances cooingly upon Gaston, offering her hand to be kissed

Ardèle My dear Gaston, what a lovely surprise! I'm so pleased to see you. I've just read your book. Such depth! Such heart! At Emilienne de Pontadour's last drinks your name was on everybody's lips. "Such a genius!" they all cried. They were tipping you for the Goncourt! I was saying to my husband only a moment ago, one has so few friends of your calibre!

Gaston (*suddenly lit up with delight, gurgling back at her as he leans over her hand*) You're too kind! Too kind, my dear lady! A humble little essay on the impossibility of human communication, nothing more!

Sudden Black-out on this picture

The Lights come up again to reveal a double bed. Night. Léon is in bed with Joséphine. They appear to be asleep, back to back. All at once Joséphine turns abruptly over. Léon gives a roar in the dark

Léon Agh!
Joséphine Now what's the mater?
Léon My foot.

Joséphine turns back the other way, in an ill humour

Joséphine It's not much fun, you know, sleeping with a gouty foot!
Léon I know. I have some experience of it. You can always go and sleep on the living-room sofa. I can't—the damned thing would come with me.
Joséphine Lovely isn't it. All you had to do was eat less! You think it's a life for anyone, being the girl-friend of an invalid?
Léon No.
Joséphine I'm twenty!
Léon (*growling in the dark*) Let's not exaggerate, now. You *used* to be twenty.
Joséphine When I met you I *was* twenty.
Léon (*correcting her*) You were twenty-four.
Joséphine You're not going to go on haggling about it, are you? When someone's twenty-four they're twenty. You're more than twice my age.

I've given you the best years of my life. And what have you done with them? You're the only one who got any benefit. (*She broods bitterly*) What have I done with my five years with you—can you tell me that?

Léon You've lived them. You've learnt to speak properly. You've been taught which fork to use. One's time is never wasted. That's a foolish expression.

Joséphine I haven't managed to get into the theatre. You were supposed to be helping me.

Léon I've done my best.

Joséphine A man in your position—you could have made them take me. I could have been a star by now! You were still a success then. You could do anything you liked!

Léon That's what they all think. But you can't do much. You might just be able to twist a producer's arm, if you catch him on a day when there's some money around, which isn't often. But not the public. There are too many of them.

Joséphine (*bitterly*) In fact it's been more of a hindrance than a help, being your girl-friend. Every time I went to an audition they'd stop me after a dozen lines—and they'd start talking about you! How were you these days, were you writing anything at the moment, etcetera—and then they'd turn me down because I wasn't right for the part.

Léon (*impenetrably*) How odd.

Joséphine It didn't stop some of the craftier ones making a pass at me, just on the offchance. They knew what a difference in age there was between us, and they thought, she didn't mind doing it with him, so who knows ...? (*Slyly*) I haven't told you that before, have I?

Léon You haven't, no.

Joséphine (*meanly*) Well, I'm telling you now. Do you want names? They're all friends of yours.

He remains unmoved. She watches him rancorously for a reaction. He breathes peacefully in the darkness

Don't you care? Are you just going to pretend to be asleep? You can't even feel pain any more, can you.

Léon (*mysteriously, in the darkness*) In my heart, no. Only in my foot.

Joséphine (*exasperated*) Oh, your foot! First it was your wife and children—now it's your foot. (*She broods rancorously*) How about my soul? Have you ever fussed over my soul?

Léon That's beside the point.

Joséphine Oh no it's not! (*She sits up and howls vehemently*) I've got a soul, you know, just as much as you! Have you thought about it sometimes?

Léon (*calmly*) You've got a soul and you've got feet, just like everyone else. But will you stop kicking them about all over the bed? You're going to do me an injury.

Joséphine (*sitting up in bed, vehemently*) I don't care! I want to shout it from the housetops. My cup is full. You can't stop it running over.

Léon (*philosophically switching on the light and settling himself comfort-*

Act I 25

ably) That takes care of the rest of the act then. Away you go, but mind my foot.

Joséphine (*getting going, wildly and volubly*) When I met you, when I was in that little set of people at drama school, I was practically a star. I'd been spotted. A very well-known film director had even told me he had me in mind for a part ... Unfortunately I couldn't have dinner with him that particular evening because my poor mother was ill—so he invited another girl from the school instead, and he was absolutely sick about it, because she was as plain as a spoon and I knew he didn't like her as much as me ... But the thing was, he could only manage that particular evening because his wife was coming home next day. I found out later he'd slept with her—not his wife—the girl—but he still hadn't given her the part. It's a very closed world, you know, films!

Léon I know.

Joséphine But that doesn't alter the fact he asked me first! A very well-known director. I won't tell you his name because I don't like to boast. "You're it!" he used to say. "You're absolutely it! If we don't get you the film's a non-starter."

Léon (*politely inquiring*) So he didn't make the film?

Joséphine (*mournfully*) Yes, he did.

Léon And who did he give the part to in the end?

Joséphine To some girl from the Comédie-Française.

Léon Oh, an actress.

Joséphine The producer was sleeping with her. Things like that always get on top of you.

Léon (*neutrally*) I suppose so.

Joséphine (*mysteriously, very casually*) I've met him again since then. This big film director—I'm not going to tell you his name. He said why didn't we have dinner anyway? Because he had another project in mind. Unfortunately by that time I knew you.

Léon (*sincerely wounded*) Why didn't you go? I've never tried to stop you eating!

Joséphine Come on, you don't wolf down some bloke's caviar and champagne only to tell him you've got a headache when you get to the dessert! I decided I was going to be faithful to you from the first moment I got involved with you, because I thought you really loved me. It's just the way I'm made—I lead with my heart. What have I got out of it, though? A part with thirty-two lines in some play that flopped—and gout!

Léon No. You had the part—I have the gout.

Joséphine (*her voice hard*) Yes, but the gout you share. Liberally. (*She exclaims furiously*) Wouldn't you believe?—I'm such a mug!

Léon (*gently*) No, no. "Would you believe?—I'm such a mug!" Or: "I'm such a mug, you wouldn't believe!"

Joséphine You're so boring! What's the difference? But that's the way it is—I'm too soft-hearted. Well, you can't make yourself into a different person. I'm a nun by nature. Only when the nun in me comes up against an egotist with a hide as thick as yours it's not surprising if I get a bit narked about it and want to tell you so. Even with a few grammatical errors—even in the middle of the night! I've got my own monologue at last! The one you've never written me! I'm supplying my own script.

Léon (*calmly*) All right. We'll see if it's any good. But mind my foot. Give the gestures a miss. Don't act—just run through it for words.

Joséphine I'll do what I like! Because if you just wanted someone to look after you then you shouldn't have hired an actress. A nurse for some old bloke who isn't even a success any more ... What a great part for someone with all the promise I had! When there are so many young directors around who are crawling with new ideas! I mean, just yesterday I met this Greek bloke in a café on the Boulevard Saint-Germain. He offered me *Phèdre*.

Léon (*beginning to sink gently into a doze. In a voice which is already rather thick with sleep*) The one by Racine?

Joséphine (*imperturbably*) Certainly. The one by Racine. By some miracle, the rights are still free. he said the play had never been done properly. No-one up to now had dared to show all the stuff in it about society. He says *Phèdre* has always been played vertically but really it's a horizontal play.

Léon (*his voice becoming more and more remote*) Horizontal ... Meaning they want to do it with everyone lying down?

Joséphine That's right! Under the weight of a repressive society that's crushing them. All the characters flat on their faces, dressed in rags, underneath this huge thing of metal girders like an iron cage that's choking the life out of them. Like in some police-state society. But that's going to cost the earth, of course, a completely bare stage. So he's looking for a subsidy. But the Government doesn't seem to understand the importance of what he's trying to say. He's in despair. Then when he discovered I knew you—and he kept very politely quiet about your plays—he said that if someone like you were to intervene personally with the Ministry of Culture. ... He said if it was the only way of getting it on he'd make do with sackcloth drapes, a bidet, and two or three dustbins. It may be my big chance going down the drain, do you realize that. This play, *Phèdre*,—it might have been written for me.

Léon starts to snore quietly

I tell you what I want to do in the theatre and you fall asleep. You're an egotist. You've never given a damn about anybody else. All you care about is what concerns you. (*She looks at him, full of dolorous rancour*) Of course, I'm just a halfwit and you're a tremendously clever man. But sometimes the halfwits know a thing or two more about life than the tremendously clever men do. You dole out money right, left and centre like a nice kind man, because you're weak, and because it's the easiest way out, and sometimes you're even a little moist-eyed. But you've never loved anyone, you dried-up old prune ... We're all just ghosts around you.

Pause. Then suddenly, disarmed and almost touching, she ends up

So what's what she's telling you, your little halfwit who's never understood anything about anything. And she's telling you it all because you're asleep and that's the only time when you take anything in ... the only time when you stop being tremendously clever, and stop believing that life is like a well-made play ...
Léon (*waking up abruptly*) Were you talking to me? I must have dozed off. What were you saying?
Joséphine Nothing. I've finished. You can turn the light off. I'm going back to sleep.
Léon (*feeling for the switch, mumbling*) All right. I'll think about it all in the morning and we'll see what we can do. And remind me in the morning about my play. After the interval I've got to have something happening ... It can't go on being all monologues ... (*He turns off the light and settles to sleep*) Oh, damn it, let's have a quick one ...
Joséphine (*waking up with a start just as she was getting to sleep*) What did you say?
Léon (*his voice thicker and thicker, like a record running down*) Nothing. I dreamt I was smoking ...

Silence. They both snore. The lights go slowly down to Black-out

CURTAIN

ACT II

The studio, as in the earlier scenes of Act I

Léon is writing at his desk. What he is writing is a cheque. Gaston is standing by the desk with his hand half held out. When he has finished writing the cheque, Léon goes on talking with the cheque in his hand, watched uneasily by Gaston

Léon There we are, then! Labiche used to say that a play is a centipede, a creature with a hundred feet that must never stand still. It's time to get the creature moving ... I've waited only too long! No more subtle references to La Rochefoucauld. No more psychological nit-picking! Trotters into the trough! (*He grimaces at an incautious move with his foot*) Agh! What one might call egocentricity at High Street prices! Something they can't pretend not to understand! Blatantly obvious devices!

Gaston (*primly, his hand half held out, his eyes fixed on the cheque*) You're going to make a spectacle of yourself, that's all.

Léon (*crying out, as he gesticulates with the cheque still in his hand*) I've done that already! Long ago! I've drained the cup of shame to the dregs! But let's keep it in perspective—I'm not Socrates and shame's not hemlock! You don't die of it. Anyway, a little success helps anything go down! I'll settle for shame and high royalties! Bring on the cuckold husband! A character of pure gold, the cuckold! Part of the French national heritage! (*He has rung while he was speaking*)

The Housekeeper appears

When Monsieur Montmachou arrives—show him straight in!

The Housekeeper exits

Now listen carefully. I always get caught out by the hard luck cases. *Les Misérables!* I end up full of self-questioning, wondering whether I've really given them everything I should. But among themselves *Les Misérables* assess each other to perfection! Very sharp-eyed they are, I can tell you! They're experts in all the dodges. And they don't like sharing their tit-bits. Very stern the poor are—when they're dealing with each other. So my idea is a simple stroke of genius. I'm going to get them to solve each other's problems. First the poor cuckolded husband. That's a very straightforward scene.

The Housekeeper shows Bernard in, then exits

Bernard! Come in!

Bernard You wanted to see me, Father-in-law?

Léon I did indeed. You know Gaston?

Bernard (*greeting him stiffly*) I believe we have ... ah ...

Gaston I think we have ... um ...

Léon (*setting to work*) My poor dear Bernard ... (*He makes a fresh start on a different note*) No! My dear Bernard ... It's Saturday ... (*He looks*

Act II

at his watch) It's two-fifteen precisely, and I have been given a little job to do that concerns you. Sit down, why don't you.

Bernard I'm rather pushed for time. My tennis partners are expecting me at the club. I've made quite a good start in the tournament. I don't want to give them a walkover.

Léon Sit down nevertheless. It'll be better if you're sitting down.

Bernard sits

(*To Gaston*) You sit down, too.

Gaston No, I'm going to leave you in peace. Clothilde is expecting me. I don't like leaving her on her own, as you know ... I don't know what she's thinking even when I'm there ... So when I'm not there ... If you could just let me have the cheque now you've written it. You've got it in your hand.

Léon Sit down first.

As Gaston hesitates, Léon cries in the voice used for a dog

Sit!

Gaston (*rebelling*) You're taking unfair advantage, as always. And your attempts at humour I can only describe as appalling. I don't know how anyone could be so lacking in taste!

Léon I do. I shall explain to you. Sit!

Gaston sits, sulkily. Léon gives him his cheque

There! Give me your paw. Good boy! I'm giving you the wherewithal for a new car, so the least you can do is a little service for me in return. After-sales service—that's what they call it in the motor trade. Bernard, Gaston needs your help.

Bernard *My* help?

Léon With some advice. You were here yesterday—you know the difficulties he has with Clothilde ... You've a wide experience of women ... You've got to help him. (*To Gaston*) Tell him your problem.

Gaston (*sourly*) I can assure you this little scene isn't funny.

Léon Not for a start, I'll give you that. It's dull. But it may develop. It's a good situation.

Gaston (*bitterly*) In your eyes.

Léon Not for the protagonists, I agree. But the author can't worry his head about that. When Polonius hides behind the arras in *Hamlet*, everyone—even people who aren't familiar with the play—they all know it's going to turn out badly for him. But it's a good situation, nonetheless. That's what the theatre's all about!

Gaston We're not in the theatre.

Léon (*sweetly*) Yes, we are. You know perfectly well we are. Explain to Bernard why you're frightened of losing Clothilde. Listen closely, Bernard—you may be able to help him.

Bernard (*looking at his watch*) Father-in-law, they are expecting me at the club, and the weekend's the only time I have for sport ...

Léon But this is going to be sport! Come on, relax both of you! You're

sitting there all stiff and suspicious! Suspicious of what, I wonder? Gaston, explain to Bernard why you're afraid of being cuckolded ...
Gaston (*wounded*) You certainly pick your words!
Léon Magic words! That particular one has been making the French laugh ever since the Middle Ages. Why deprive ourselves of it? Come on, now, unbutton a little! We're among friends. What's the matter with your Clothilde? Worried about something, is she?
Gaston (*sulkily*) Yes. She's worrying about something.
Léon Listen carefully, Bernard. Take notes. Have you got a pencil? So what's she worried about, my old hearty?
Gaston She feels she's not achieving complete selfhood.
Léon She feels she's not achieving complete selfhood. Listen carefully, Bernard.
Bernard (*stiffly*) I'm not an intellectual, Father-in-law! "Complete selfhood". I don't understand what the expression means.
Léon Nor do I. Nor, probably, do the women who use it. To employ a more down-to-earth expression—and one that women are equally fond of—Clothilde doesn't know who she is. (*To Gaston*) Is that right?
Gaston Yes. Clothilde doesn't know who she is.
Léon You may possibly feel that there's not much chance of her being anyone *else* ... But there we are, she's not absolutely certain whether it's her or not. Because, like a lot of women nowadays, she needs, or so she says, to find herself. Is that right, Gaston?
Gaston Yes. She needs to find herself.
Bernard (*stiffly*) I still don't understand.
Léon I'll translate for you, Bernard. The truth of the matter—and this is the source of the anguish that our friend Gaston feels, this is why he's afraid of losing her—the truth of the matter, in plain language, is that Clothilde is bored out of her mind with Gaston.
Gaston (*crying out*) I'm not going to let you get away with that! Clothilde is terribly sensitive—she's someone who's been flayed alive, who feels pain at the slightest thing—that's all. I give her everything I can—
Léon (*correcting him*) Everything *we* can ...
Gaston (*giving him a dirty look*) —but it's no good, it's never enough for her. Clothilde is a little poor girl who had a very unhappy childhood. Then she was so traumatized by her first four husbands, who were all absolute brutes, that she's bound to be a little thin-skinned. The slightest thing hurts her! We love each other deeply, and we have a physical relationship of very high quality—and yet I feel that she eludes me. I feel I'm not giving her enough.
Léon He feels he's giving her everything, and yet he fears he is not giving her enough. You have a wife yourself, Bernard ... In your opinion is he giving her enough, or not enough?
Bernard (*pontificating as always, rather ridiculously*) More important than what one gives is the way in which one gives it ...
Léon Quite so. Corneille. But what's your personal opinion, Bernard?
Bernard (*to Gaston*) It seems perfectly straightforward to me. She's your wife, is she?

Act II

Gaston Well, she will be shortly.
Bernard Your lawful wife?
Gaston Well, shortly, thanks to ... (*He stops*)
Bernard It all seems clear enough, then. You'll have children—I hope you'll have children—they'll keep you on an even keel—and you'll have a home. She will be the guardian of your home, and her task there will be to wait for you and to make your life as pleasant as possible when you come back in the evening, exhausted after a hard day's work. That is where she will "find herself", if she insists on the expression. My own wife, splendid woman that she is, has got that firmly into her head. That's why she "knows who she is", as you put it, and why I do too. No problems. I hope you'll be as happy as I am. One word of advice: be firm. Never show doubt. Women need certainty and firmness. (*He gets up*) Will you excuse me, Father-in-law? My partners are expecting me at the club. I'm on court at quarter past three.
Léon (*looking at his watch and sighing*) Saturday, two-thirty p.m. Autumn's here. The days are drawing in, and a weekend is so quickly gone. Sit down, Bernard, we're not through yet.
Bernard (*looking at his watch in some annoyance and sitting down on the edge of the chair*) Very well. Five minutes, but no longer. I don't want to lose this start I've got.
Léon (*struck by this*) I beg your pardon? Lose this tart you've got? Is that any way to speak of her?
Bernard This start I've got in the tournament. I told you. I very much want to hang on to this really rather goodish start.
Léon (*with a heartrending cry*) Oh! Don't tempt me with easy puns! You know I'm only too prone to them, and I'll get myself ticked off again! Bernard, you have already lost this tart of yours. (*He takes the plunge*) My daughter has a lover!
Bernard (*loftily*) What's that supposed to do with me?
Léon (*slightly surprised in spite of himself*) Oh, well, that's fine. I see you're taking it very well.
Bernard (*going right on*) Marie-Christine runs after anything in trousers. She can get herself divorced again if she likes. It's nothing to do with me.
Léon (*groaning miserably*) No, no, Bernard! We're not talking about Marie-Christine! I've two daughters—you're forgetting! We're talking about Lucie!
Bernard My wife?
Léon Exactly.
Bernard (*smiling*) Impossible.
Léon Why impossible?
Bernard (*crisply*) She worships me.
Léon (*with another groan*) I'm afraid she doesn't.
Bernard I'm afraid she does. We're a perfect couple, as you well know.
Léon I'm afraid not. Not perfect at all, my poor dear Bernard.
Bernard My wife—being unfaithful? I'd like to see it!
Léon (*unhappily*) I'm afraid you're going to see it, Bernard, as of Monday!
Bernard (*exclaiming*) Why would Lucie be unfaithful? It's a ridiculous

notion. I've given her everything; my name, a comfortable home, two children, my regard. She'd have to be an absolute rotter! What are you driving at with this tasteless joke of yours?

Gaston (*unable to prevent himself crying out*) You see!

Léon See what?

Gaston Your lack of taste! I'm not the only one to remark upon it. I agree with your son-in-law—you say the first thing that comes into your head! You see the worst in everything! That, incidentally, is the basis of your dubious success in the theatre.

Léon (*with a woebegone gesture*) It's not me, my poor loves—it's the facts that are lacking in taste. And painful as it may be, we must look truth's bare backside in the face! It's not just on the beach that the ladies show off their hindquarters now. Their bodies are their own, and they can do as they like with them! (*To Gaston*) You're not going to deny that Clothilde was out all night last night? You were just telling me that you wondered where she'd been. (*To Bernard*) His wife didn't sleep at home last night. Where was she? That is the question, as they say in a certain English play that you may not have had the occasion to read.

Gaston She was crying on the shoulder of this girl she knows. She just felt so miserable. She told me when she got back at lunchtime.

Léon (*to Bernard*) Does that seem reasonable to you, Bernard? You're a shrewd observer of human psychology. A woman has a jolly dinner with her chums, then suddenly feels so miserable that she can't manage to come back and cry in her own home?

Bernard (*with a little superior smile*) There does seem to me to be something a little unusual here...

Gaston (*stung*) Unusual? Why unusual? The heart has its reasons...

Léon (*interrupting him*) ... that reason knows nothing of. Right. Pascal. Let Bernard have his say.

Bernard I don't want to be impertinent, but if I were in your shoes...

Léon (*seizing on this*) Exactly! If you were in his shoes, Bernard...?

Bernard (*not without a certain irony*) I have to confess that I should at least feel a little uneasy... But as I said before, the way these modern young women behave is a closed book to me. Now my wife is never unhappy. She has her little outbursts, as everyone does. But she has them at home. I'm the one who consoles her.

Léon And does she have them often, these little outbursts?

Bernard (*shrugging*) Nerves, nerves. With the kind of life we lead today we all live on our nerves. Nothing serious, though. She knows she can rely on my being there!

Léon That's just the trouble—your being there! There's a rather nice story about Lucien Guitry, the old actor. One day he was beating his mistress in a cab, and when she bellowed "Help! Help!!" out of the window he tried to calm her by shouting: "Don't worry! I'm here!"

Bernard I don't see the connection.

Gaston (*sourly*) More of your boulevard wit! You'd sell your mother if you could get a gag out of it!

Léon Not mine, that one. I merely quote. We must take the plunge. Hom-

Act II

eopathic remedies have not availed us. There's nothing for it but radical surgery. Bernard, do you know one Roméro?
Bernard Roméro Putillani? He's one of my friends at the club.
Léon But he's not in the tournament with you?
Bernard No, he's away on a business trip this weekend. Though he's not in the tournament in any case, because he went out after the start.
Léon (*woefully*) Did he? He went out after this ...? Oh, don't tempt me! Don't tempt me, Bernard! I should have liked this scene to be more delicately handled. Because it's a serious matter, after all. We laugh at men being deceived, but it's a hateful thing ... Its other name is being alone ... And being alone is man's one true sickness. Of being alone, alone we die. Because then a man is left confronting himself, and himself is a man he can't abide. (*He takes the plunge*) Well then. Lucie has given me the task of telling you that she is in love with your friend Roméro. She wants to get divorced and go and live with him. (*He mops his brow with his handkerchief*) Whew! It's warm this afternoon, don't you think?

There is a rather long silence. Gaston makes a move towards the door in embarrassment

Gaston Thank you for the cheque ... I think I'd better go back now and find Clothilde ... I *am* a little worried, as I'm sure you appreciate ...

His voice trails away. He looks at Bernard, who remains stiff and unmoving, and who says merely

Bernard Divorce is not the practice of the Montmachous.
Léon But since, as I've just explained, she *wants*—
Bernard (*more and more stiffly*) And there are some explanations we never have. We say nothing, and we respond with silences. That's how families are kept together ... Do you really imagine that in all the years since the thirteenth century we haven't had our cuckolds, like everybody else? There were the wars—and we fought in all of them—crusades were our profession. But read our family chronicles; never was there any suspicion cast upon the honour of our womenfolk. Not even in the eighteenth century, under the Regency, when the morals of the best of families wavered a little. Mishaps there may have been, but a blind eye was always turned. It's a question of principles. (*He makes a move towards the door*) Good-day, gentlemen. I attach some importance to this little competition of ours at the club, and I'm afraid I may miss the ... beginning.
Léon (*a little unnerved in spite of himself*) But what's going to happen?
Bernard Nothing's going to happen. All I ask of your daughter is to behave correctly. Appearances largely suffice to make a family. You should realize that, as a man of the theatre ...
Léon (*groaning*) But what about me—what am I going to tell my daughter on Monday? You're putting me in a rather awkward position. You have to think about other people as well!
Bernard Tell her what I've just told you. If she has a little breeding she'll understand.

Léon (*rather flabbergasted*) My dear Bernard, I've underestimated you. You're tougher than I thought.
Bernard No. But I have certain traditions behind me. It's about all we have left. You've always taken me for a fool, I'm well aware of that. The Montmachous *are* fools, the lot of them, and they're proud of the fact. My only mistake—but I was young at the time, which may be some excuse—was the misalliance I made by marrying the daughter of some clever strolling player ... My mother warned me, though. "One doesn't marry people like that", she said. "They have a habit of thinking, and that always leads to trouble." I should have married the daughter of some fool with the same background. People ought to marry among themselves. I made a mistake. I am paying for it. The Montmachous always settle their debts.
Gaston (*babbling, flabbergasted*) And you don't even feel any pain? I'm as big-hearted as they come, but if I discovered that Clothilde ...
Bernard (*stiffly*) That's my business ...
Gaston Yes, but really ...
Bernard The Montmachous don't give interviews.
Léon There are some awkward situations in which one is driven back upon the dullest of commonplaces ... My poor dear Bernard. Perhaps you were asking too much of her?
Bernard (*giving a sudden unguarded cry, for all his stiffness*) What did I ask that was so much beyond her? I asked her to devote herself to me. To be the woman I needed. The woman I had always imagined at my side ... Good God, isn't it an ideal to be a man's wedded wife? To wear his family jewels, to bear his name, to be the mother of his children? You're suggesting that she was bored. I've had to work. The Montmachous have long since fallen on evil days. Do you think I enjoy being at the factory? The only things I enjoy are riding, hunting, and tennis. (*In all sincerity*) I devote every weekend to them, certainly: but she could always come to the club and watch me play. It's true that when I get home in the evening I don't feel like going out again, since I've only just come in. Nor like making pretty little speeches, when I've been making pretty little speeches all day ... What is happiness, anyway? It's a shopgirls' philosophy! She had her home, her children, her position! (*He advances upon Léon*) And she had respect! But what does respect mean to you?
Léon (*terrified*) To me? Nothing. Mind my foot!
Bernard (*icily*) Nothing. I'm afraid that's right. (*He resumes*) I respected her. She had become a Montmachou. A Montmachou she will remain, and I shall continue to respect her in the eyes of the world, in spite of this Italian. All I ask of her is to keep up appearances—and to keep her mouth shut. Silence—it's a very ancient remedy. But people have forgotten it. Nowadays everyone says everything. We have become a world of washerwomen. And things aren't made any better by television. (*He broods nonetheless. Angrily*) But with some greasy Levantine! And she a Montmachou!
Léon (*protesting timidly*) That's not quite right. It's no excuse, I know, but in fact he's not exactly a Levantine ... He's an Italian.

Act II

Bernard (*with a bitter and derisive laugh*) Ha! My grandfather—who was generally reckoned to be a fool, too—even in our circles, where we're rather broadminded about it—my grandfather always used to say to me—and I see now he was a man above other men—he used to say: "Below the Loire, my boy, watch out—they're all blackamoors!" (*Flatly*) Where are your family from?
Léon (*modestly*) From Châteauroux. Just slightly below.
Bernard I should have guessed. Good-day, gentlemen.

He goes out, as stiffly as ever

Léon (*mopping his brow*) I'm sweating! I'm sure I've got a temperature. Anyway, that's the last time I do other people's dirty work for them! I'd have thought it would have been a funnier scene. A cuckolded husband, after all—that's a surefire winner ...! But you can't rely on anything in the theatre these days!
Gaston (*thoughtfully*) He's being very noble about it, though!
Léon (*sombrely*) Yes ... He's being very noble about it. It's another way of being egotistical. There are quite a number ... I'm noble about things, too—it suits my style. I've got the trick of it. Man has a prodigious instinct for self-preservation. The truth is that he never loved his wife. All he loved, like everybody else, was the idea he had of her inside his head. He'll be all right; he'll manage to look out for Number One. (*Suddenly he cries out, clownishly inspired*) Number One! The magic number, that unlocks the secret of the universe. *Number One.* That's not a bad title. (*He takes the thermometer from his desk*)
Gaston Speak for yourself. You've always been dead to all feeling. Whereas I've spent my life being crushed by other people's sufferings. All my life I've been giving, giving.
Léon (*with a thermometer in his mouth*) Who to?
Gaston Well, to you, for a start! And then to women, to all the women I've loved!
Léon (*chewing on his thermometer, mockingly*) You must be exhausted!
Gaston Shall I tell you something? I've never told this to anyone, not even to you. When I was ten my mother went off with a dentist. She left Papa and me. I'm just an abandoned little boy—and I've been looking for my mother ever since ... (*Suddenly he adds, moist-eyed*) That's why, when we were at primary school in our little blue check pinafores, I got so attached to you. You'd become my mother!
Léon (*taken aback in spite of himself, removing the thermometer from his mouth*) Now you're stretching it a bit. (*He reads the thermometer*) Over a hundred. I thought so!

Enter the Housekeeper, looking as usual like the bearer of ill tidings

Léon barks at her

What is it now, Madame Boudard? You can see I'm dangerously ill.
Housekeeper Message from your wife. Urgent. Sent her maid with it. Apparently she's dying, she can't get out of bed, she's suddenly got some fatal disease, and you'll have to go right away if you want to see her

alive ... Well, that's if I've got it right, because the girl was jabbering it all in Spanish. (*She goes straight on, holding out a paper*) And here's the plumber's estimate. Twenty thousand. And they say they've got to have half of it now if you want them to start in the morning. If not they're off to another job. Apparently the whole district's leaking! Meanwhile there's no water. I've had to go and get some next door to do my carrots.

Léon (*with sudden calm*) Right. The main thing is to keep calm. No excitement, the doctor told me. I'll make out a cheque for the plumber, and I'll limp off on my one good paw to see my dying wife! I may be an egotist, but I'm an egotist who's devoted to others. It's still the easiest way to get a little peace and quiet.

He writes the cheque, while the Housekeeper waits for it with outstretched hand. Gaston seizes the chance to slip discreetly away. Léon notices and cries

Hey! Don't you go running away! You're coming with me. You can't abandon your mother at a time like this. You can hold on to the corner of her pinny while she talks to the poor sick lady!

Enter Ardèle. She is pale and gaunt and is leaning on a stick

Ardèle (*solemnly*) Since I thought you wouldn't so much as lift a finger I got myself up and brought myself here to die. By your side. In the marriage bed.
Léon The marriage bed! (*He runs to guard the bedroom door*) Hell's bloody bells! This is my private apartment you're in. I'm a free man, do you understand? I'm a free man!
Ardèle Yes. But wherever there's a bed for two with you inside it, that's the marriage bed and I am entitled to be in it beside you—because I am your wife!
Léon (*howling*) Supposing I have my heart attack! Supposing I'm felled to the ground, right here in front of you!
Ardèle (*with dignity*) Then I shall find the strength, sick as I am, to get up and nurse you.
Léon (*dropping into an armchair, defeated*) This is appalling!
Gaston (*sententiously*) No, it's not. It's Roman! Seneca's wife!
Léon Why, what did she do?
Gaston Kept her husband company to the last, by slitting her own veins when he slit his.

Sudden Black-out

When the Lights come up again Léon is lying on the chaise-longue. The Doctor is at the desk

Doctor Annoyances like that obviously don't help matters ... So what happened to your wife, to get to the end of the story?
Léon An absolute bolt from the blue! Yesterday afternoon my friend Gaston Lepied, who no-one thought had the slightest chance, got the Prix Goncourt for his latest novel ... The jury, by dint of all their efforts to block each other, ended up on the twenty-seventh round by giving the palm to the feeblest contender. But luckily for me there was

Act II

a very grand drinks party today given by Emilienne de Pontadour to celebrate the occasion. My wife, who's got her nose into everything, simply couldn't miss such a Parisian event. She found she was completely cured all of a sudden, and off she went for a good yatter, bravely overcoming her fatal disease, whatever that may have been. Whereupon I had the locks changed.

Doctor (*putting his apparatus away*) Wise move. Protect yourself from your family. You're back up to one hundred and seventy over ninety-eight.

Léon (*humbly*) Is that still high?

Doctor (*coldly*) Good heavens, yes. (*Suddenly bantering*) Aren't you going to feel my pulse today, then? We fellow-practitioners must look after each other!

Léon (*morosely*) No, I'm not. It's every man on his own now. Physician, heal thyself!

Doctor (*looking through his laboratory reports*) I must also tell you that all the tests I got back this morning are bad. How about the cholesterol? Do you ever think about the cholesterol?

Léon (*grumpily*) No, I don't. I can't think about everything.

The Doctor takes another glance at the reports

Doctor It's quite funny, though. You've got this bad attack of gout, and yet the lab reports are quite categoric: you've no uric acid. None in the urine and none in the blood.

Léon (*a gleam of hope in his eye*) That could be a good sign?

Doctor (*flatly*) No. It must be concealing something worse. Anyway, it's extremely interesting.

Léon For whom?

Doctor For medical science. I shall write a paragraph or two about it for the journals. It must have some connection with the heart business. I'll have a word with Abject about it. Have you seen him as I asked?

Léon No, I haven't. I rang and his receptionist gave me an appointment in six weeks' time.

Doctor (*with a sour little laugh*) Ah, yes! He's a terribly busy fellow! What we're looking at there is a dazzling medical success story!

Léon In the treatment of heart disease?

Doctor In the treatment of his career. This is a chap who ten years ago arrived in Paris barefoot, or pretty nearly. And shall I tell you how he made his reputation? This will make you laugh. You know Gustave Chancrard? The big sugar man?

Léon Only by name. Why, was *he* eating too much of it?

Doctor Not at all. He'd been put on saccharine for his diabetes years before. But he was selling too much of it. Huge corporation—multinational interests. That's what was killing him, like all these big businessmen ... Wait for it—you'll love this. A real Parisian story. Professor Piedeloup, who was treating him for his heart, breaks his leg one winter at Saint-Moritz. So instead he sends round Abject, who was his assistant at the time. Now Abject is a good-looking chap, and Chancrard's young wife, who used to be a model, takes a colossal fancy to him. He becomes her lover. And so as to be undisturbed with his ladyfriend between five and six, he prescribes the old man two hours cycling with his valet every afternoon in the Bois de Boulogne. The wife, meanwhile, her senses gratified by Abject's embraces, suddenly starts to leave her ageing tycoon in peace, and there at a stroke is good old Chancrard cured! Since then the whole of Paris has sworn by Abject, and Abject alone! Isn't that funny? It doesn't seem to be making you laugh.

Léon (*humbly*) Perhaps *I* should take up cycling?

Doctor Certainly not. It would kill you. Your heart would never stand it. It should have killed *him*, by the way—but instead it cured him. I'll tell you a secret. We don't know everything! But we sometimes have a stroke of luck—and when nature does the trick, fortunately we get the credit. (*Suddenly he broods bitterly*) Not that *I've* ever had any luck. I'm just marking time. I don't kill any more patients than the others—I sometimes even cure them. But I'm not all the rage, like Abject! It's all so hit-and-miss. Luck's half the game in medicine, just like in everything else. Look at your friend Gaston Lepied and his windfall in the Goncourt. His name's on everyone's lips this morning! I've asked my receptionist to get it for me.

Léon What?

Doctor Your friend's book. You're my third call today, and it comes up every time. I couldn't talk about it; I was so embarrassed! I looked a complete fool in front of all my lovely ladies! Unbutton your top, so we can listen to this heart of yours.

Léon I've taken my temperature. I was still over a hundred this morning.

Doctor (*applying his stethoscope*) Normal feverish reaction. It's not a type of modern literature that I greatly care for. But after all, one has to keep up ... I have a largely female practice, and these ladies are all highly aroused by your friend's book. When you finally get the point, I gather, it's hideously obscene! If it's obscure and filthy it should go down like a bomb in Paris! Ah, Paris! It'll always be the same! Vanity, sex, and money! (*He straightens up and puts his instruments away*)

Léon What about my heart?

Doctor (*lightly*) That's still the same, too. Rest. Complete rest! No shocks or surprises. Anyway, I notice that in spite of your temperature you've lost a lot of your aggressiveness. You don't look as if you want to set upon me today.

Léon You think this calm mood is good news?

Doctor (*laughing*) It is for me! (*He grows serious again*) But we'll have to keep an eye on it. If you go on being low I'll give you some Perlinpin.

Léon (*suspiciously*) Perlinpin? What's that?

Doctor A helicoidal derivate of menoposexilagate, combined with a small dose of metanoxyl-diphasic acid. They're getting amazing results with it in America.

Léon How about in France? I'm patriotic, whatever anyone says; my heart's French.

Doctor I told you—it's completely new. They're still experimenting. But

Act II

the figures from the hospitals are encouraging. There are serious side-effects naturally. That's why we have to be very careful. Don't take more than a quarter of a tablet per day. If you collapse, of course, give me a ring.
Léon If I can.
Doctor (*lightly*) Obviously, it would all be much more convenient if you were in hospital!
Léon Much more convenient for whom?
Doctor For me. Anyway, I'll get you a nurse to keep an eye on things.
Léon (*with a thin smile*) At least get me a pretty one! I hate plain Janes. It makes me ill to look at them.
Doctor (*sourly*) A plain Jane is precisely what you'll get. Plain Janes are the only sort I employ. It's better for the health. And you'll have to behave in that department, of course. You take my meaning? You share the bed with your young friend?
Léon I do.
Doctor From now on she'll sleep in here, on this thing.
Léon You'll have to tell her yourself. Her feelings are very easily hurt.
Doctor (*writing out his prescription*) I'll put it on the prescription. You're in the hands of the medical profession now, and you'll have to watch your step! Just because we don't know what's wrong with you yet—that doesn't mean we're going to let you do whatever you like ...! In any case, we'll have more elaborate tests done on you and in the end we'll put our finger on it. We've got ways of doing it now, with biopsies. You work the lucky fellow over—you take little bits and pieces of everything. You analyse them, and in the end you always get there. Intuitive diagnosis went out with top hats and sidewhiskers!
Léon What if you *don't* put your finger on it?
Doctor (*lightly*) There's always the autopsy. We've got more than one trick up our sleeve! All right, then. I've got four more patients to see after you. I spend my life sitting in cars ... As a matter of fact I've got a new one—marvellous—American job ... What sort have you got at the moment?
Léon (*morosely*) I don't have one.
Doctor Lucky man! you don't know how fortunate you are! You don't have the same professional obligations as me, so do everything you can on foot. At the double, if possible! Jogging—that's the secret of good health! We've discovered that now.
Léon On foot?
Doctor Right.
Léon At the double?
Doctor Whenever you can.
Léon Jogging?
Doctor That's it!
Léon What about this?
Doctor What's that?
Léon My foot.
Doctor Oh, that. Is it still giving you pain?

Léon Yes, it is.
Doctor Perfectly normal. What do you expect? You've got gout, old chap!
Léon (*protestingly*) But if I've got no uric acid!
Doctor (*putting his hair to rights, ready to leave*) You're not going to blame that on me, are you? It's not my fault if you've no uric acid! You *ought* to have some—that's the long and short of it! It would be vastly simpler—we'd know where we were. I'll tell you something worth remembering: in medicine it doesn't pay to try and stand out from the crowd. We have cases of this, we have cases of that. We've studied them. We treat them. Let's stick to that. It's not a self-service grocery, you know, medicine! If you'd had uric acid in your blood I'd have cured your gout by now. But, no, you want to be the one and only. (*In a hurry now, he claps Léon cordially on the shoulder*) All right, then! I'll see you the day after tomorrow. We'll take a look at that foot of yours ... Perhaps it ought to come off.

Léon reacts

I'm beginning to wonder if there's not something wrong with my carburettor. You complain about doctors; do you think mechanics are any better? We all have our problems, old chap!

He goes cheerfully out

Léon (*alone, exclaims bitterly*) The bastard! He was pretending to listen to my heart—and all the time he was just thinking about his damned carburettor. (*He broods for a moment*) We're alone in the world. We've only one friend, and alas we have to leave him. (*He pulls a sudden face. His foot is hurting*) Agh! My foot! Sickness and death—that's my real subject matter, when you come down to it. It's the ultimate in egocentricity; you're all alone with your sickness, you can't think of anything else, and other people, who have loomed so large in your life, grow strangely blurred around you. (*He grimaces*) I don't like other people, when you really come down to it. You always die alone. And you have to do it for yourself.

Just then there is a commotion outside

Gaston (*yelping; off*) No, no, no! We won't be disturbing him! I'm his friend! His one and only friend! Bring us some glasses, Madame Boudard, and come and have a drink with us!

In bursts Gaston, in a merry and triumphant mood, carrying two bottles of champagne. He is followed by Joséphine, dressed to kill. She is very excited too

(*Radiantly*) Triumph, old son!
Joséphine Triumph!
Gaston Triumph all along the line! You should have seen the mob at Emilienne de Pontadour's! But that didn't stop me thinking of my old pal! I swiped a couple of bottles of champagne from the buffet, then I quietly slipped away with Joséphine here. We're going back in ten min-

utes. There are reporters looking for me everywhere—but I just wanted to have a drink with you to celebrate! I pictured you all on your own, worrying about the result, a sick, embittered man ... I met Joséphine at the buffet and I said to her, "Joséphine, my poppet! We'll slip away, just you and I. We'll go and celebrate all this with him! I'm sure he's even happier than I am about my success! His friend, his old friend, whose talent has been finally recognized!" You're deeply moved, aren't you. You're too happy to speak!

Léon As you see.

There is further commotion outside

Ardèle (*off, excited*) Is he here? He's here, isn't he!
Housekeeper (*off*) Yes. But he doesn't want to see you.
Léon Oh, no! That's all we needed!
Ardèle (*off*) Don't be silly. Of course he wants to see me! Where is he?
Léon Keep her out! Keep her out!
Gaston Let her in, Madame Boudard! Let them all in! In here, dear lady!

Enter Ardèle

Ardèle I knew it!
Gaston You've tracked me down!
Ardèle I said to Emilienne de Pontadour, "I know where he's gone!"
Gaston We've waited so long for this moment, Léon and I.
Ardèle Straight to his old friend's bedside! (*To Léon*) You might have made the effort, just for once! But no, he has to make himself humble and come to you!
Gaston Humility is a pleasure, I assure you.

Enter the Housekeeper with a tray of glasses

Champagne, dear lady! Champagne all round! (*To Léon*) Here, this'll rout the gout! This'll give that foot of yours a hand! (*To Joséphine*) Champagne, my poppet!
Joséphine I've had five glasses already! I don't know *where* I am!
Ardèle And who is this?
Gaston This is –... ah ...

Léon groans

Ardèle But of course, you were telling us! You're going to be married!
Joséphine Are we?
Ardèle "Are we?" Oh, but you're enchanting, my dear! (*To Léon*) Isn't she utterly enchanting?
Léon Utterly.
Ardèle Such a lucky man! A wonderful prize, a charming bride! (*To Léon*) Isn't he a lucky man?
Léon Isn't he just.
Ardèle (*to Gaston*) Always so grudging about other people's good fortune! Always so graceless!
Gaston (*to Léon*) I should have thought this was just the kind of scene you

liked! (*To Ardèle*) It's just the kind of scene he writes! (*To Léon*) An old farceur like you! Why don't you sit back and enjoy it?

Enter Lucie and Bernard

Housekeeper Two more!
Gaston Two more characters!
Ardèle Lucie!
Gaston (*to Lucie*) Champagne!
Ardèle My dear Bernard!
Gaston (*to Bernard*) Champagne!
Ardèle You're just in time to offer Monsieur Lepied your congratulations!
Gaston More champagne, Madame Boudard?
Joséphine He's got some in the kitchen!

Exit the Housekeeper

Lucie What are we celebrating?
Ardèle You haven't heard?
Bernard Heard what?
Gaston A modest reward for effort, nothing more.
Bernard Oh, yes. (*To Joséphine, assuming that she is the modest reward*) So pleased to meet you. My congratulations to both of you.
Ardèle But he's won the Goncourt! Your father's oldest friend! Your father's only friend!
Lucie Where is Papa?
Ardèle (*indicating Léon*) Quite overcome by emotion.

Enter the Housekeeper with more champagne

Gaston Champagne!
Joséphine Champagne!
Housekeeper There's more of them coming up the stairs.
Gaston Send them all in!

Exit the Housekeeper

Lucie (*to Léon*) You didn't tell him!
Léon Didn't tell whom?
Lucie Bernard!
Léon I didn't know he was interested in literature.
Lucie Did you or did you not tell him what I told you to tell him?
Léon Oh. That. I did.
Bernard Your father told me nothing I find worthy of recall. Did you, Father-in-law?
Léon Didn't I?
Lucie You'll have to tell him today, then!
Bernard Tell her there are some things I shall never recall being told.
Ardèle (*to Léon*) Will you tell us all what this is about?
Lucie Tell her to keep out of this!

Enter Marie-Christine

Act II 43

Marie-Christine Tell him he'll have to pay for it! Where's Father? (*To Léon*) Tell him it was Tony's car! Tell him he shouldn't have insisted on driving it if he wasn't insured.
Gaston Champagne!
Joséphine (*giving Marie-Christine champagne*) Champagne!

Enter Arthur

Arthur Tell her it wasn't my fault!
Gaston Champagne!
Joséphine (*giving Arthur champagne*) Champagne!
Ardèle Arthur!
Arthur (*to Léon*) Tell her it was this other idiot who suddenly swung out from the kerb!

Enter the Doctor

Doctor (*to Léon*) Tell them that was a brand-new car!
Gaston Champagne! (*He gives the Doctor a glass*)
Doctor Tell them I'm going to sue them for every franc they possess!
Joséphine Who are all these people?
Gaston I don't know! But what a scene for the old farcemonger!
Lucie (*to Léon*) Tell him!
Bernard (*to Léon*) Tell her!
Marie-Christine (*to Léon*) You'll have to tell him!
Arthur (*to Léon*) You'll have to tell her!
Doctor (*to Léon*) Will you tell them!
Gaston Champagne! Champagne!
Ardèle (*to Léon, screaming*) Will you tell your children there is an innocent young girl here who is about to be married? Will you tell them they're giving her a terrible impression of family life!

Enter the Housekeeper

Housekeeper (*to Léon*) Will you tell her to keep her voice down! The neighbours are complaining!
Ardèle (*to Léon*) Will you let her talk to me like that?
All (*together, to Léon*) Tell him! Tell her! *etc.*

Léon gets up and crosses to the desk

Joséphine Look at him! He's not listening!

They all look at Léon. He is studying the sheet of paper on which he wrote his title

Léon (*reflectively*) Les Misérables ...
Gaston What's he doing?

Léon crumples up the page and begins writing with determination on a fresh one

Léon Number One. A play in two acts. Act One ... (*And he continues to write, fluently and effortlessly*)

Lucie He's writing his play.
Ardèle He's writing about us again!
Arthur Always the same, isn't it?
Marie-Christine He's putting us all in a play and making it come out to suit himself.
Gaston Wonderful! What a scene for the old Punch-and-Judy Man.
Ardèle (*to Gaston*) He'll be putting you in, don't you worry! You'll have to stop him!
Gaston Stop him? Me?
Ardèle You're his friend! You're his fellow-writer! You're the winner of the Prix Goncourt!
Lucie (*to Gaston*) Tell him to tell her...
Marie-Christine (*to Gaston*) Tell him to tell him...!
Arthur (*to Gaston*) Tell him to tell *her*...!
Doctor (*to Gaston*) Tell him to tell *them*...!
Gaston Don't all turn on *me*! What's happening?
Joséphine You're the one with the influence now! You're the one with the money!
Marie-Christine Yes! Twenty thousand francs, and I could get the car fixed before Tony sees it!
Doctor Twenty thousand francs, and I could get *my* car fixed!
Joséphine Twenty thousand francs, and I could play Phèdre!
Gaston Get away from me! Get away! What's happening?

Ardèle indicates Léon, who is busy writing

Ardèle It's him! *He's* doing it! He's taking his revenge again!
Christine (*to Gaston*) Twenty thousand! Twenty thousand!
Lucie (*to Gaston*) Tell him!
Bernard (*to Gaston*) Tell her!
Doctor (*to Gaston*) Twenty thousand!
Arthur (*to Gaston*) *I* could do with twenty thousand!
Joséphine (*to Gaston*) Twenty thousand! Twenty thousand!
Housekeeper (*to Gaston*) Keep them quiet! Shut them up!
Ardèle (*to Gaston*) Stop him! Stop him!

Gaston retreats towards the door, beset by supplicants

Gaston (*to Léon*) You wait! My next book! You'll be in it! I'll kill you in it! You'll die in agony! Agh! (*He begins to hobble*) You've given me gout! I'll give you rabies!

Gaston, pursued by Lucie, Bernard, Arthur, Marie-Christine, Doctor, House-keeper and Ardèle make for the door

All (*as they exit*) Twenty thousand! Twenty thousand! Tell him! Tell her! Tell them!... etc.

They exit

Ardèle (*shouting after Gaston*) You fool! Paralyse his hand!

Act II

Exit Ardèle after the others

Léon is left alone on stage. He stops and looks over what he has written

Léon (*reading*) "Exit his wife after the others. Léon is left alone on stage. He stops and looks over what he has written." (*He starts to write again*) "Inspiration comes to him..."

Enter the Housekeeper

Léon stops writing

Housekeeper There's a leak in the bathroom. The wall's completely sodden and next door's going to be complaining again, not to mention downstairs, because if it goes on like this they're going to have it pissing down...

Léon buries his head in his hands

CURTAIN

FURNITURE AND PROPERTY LIST

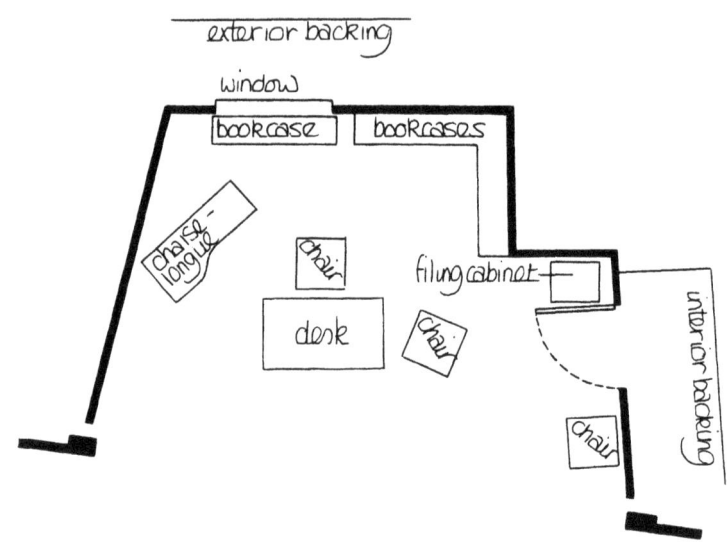

ACT I

On stage: Desk. *On it:* telephone, papers, pens, pad of paper, bell, decanter of whisky, glass, ashtray, cheque-book
Chair
Bookcases. *On shelves:* books
Chaise-longue
Several chairs
Filing cabinet
Rugs on floor
Pictures, mirror on wall

Off stage: Letters (**Housekeeper**)
Overcoat, bag containing medical instruments including sphygomomanometer, stethoscope, disposable syringes, ampoules (**Doctor**)

Personal: **Léon:** walking-stick, bandage on foot, cigarettes and lighter in pocket
Doctor: wrist-watch
Lucie: handbag with cigarettes, lighter
Gaston: cigarettes, lighter, tube of pills

During black-out on p 23 set bed and bed light

ACT II

Strike: Bed
Set: Thermometer on desk
Off stage: Estimate (**Housekeeper**)
Bag with instruments as before, plus laboratory reports, prescription pad, pen (**Doctor**)
2 bottles champagne (**Gaston**)
Tray of glasses (**Housekeeper**)
Bottle of champagne (**Housekeeper**)
Personal: **Léon:** wrist-watch, walking-stick, handkerchief
Bernard: wrist-watch
Adèle: walking-stick

LIGHTING PLOT

Practical fittings required: bed-light
Interior. An attic studio and bedroom

ACT I

To open:	General interior lighting	
Cue 1	**Léon:** "... that broke so easily, Doctor?" *Black-out*	(Page 8)
Cue 2	When ready *Bring up general interior lighting*	(Page 8)
Cue 3	**Léon:** "My dear Bernard..." *Black-out*	(Page 15)
Cue 4	When ready *Bring up general interior lighting*	(Page 15)
Cue 5	**Gaston:** "... of human communication, nothing more!" *Black-out*	(Page 23)
Cue 6	When ready *Bring up dim lighting on double bed*	(Page 23)
Cue 7	**Léon** switches on bed-light *Snap on bed-light*	(Page 24)
Cue 8	**Léon** switches off bed-light *Snap off bed-light*	(Page 27)
Cue 9	**Léon** and **Joséphine** both snore *Slowly fade to black-out*	(Page 27)

ACT II

To open:	General interior lighting	
Cue 10	**Gaston:** "... when he slit his." *Black-out*	(Page 36)
Cue 11	When ready *Bring up general interior lighting*	(Page 36)

EFFECTS PLOT

ACT I

Cue 1   **Léon:** "... somebody else's house."   (Page 3)
Telephone rings

Cue 2   **Housekeeper** exits   (Page 10)
Telephone rings

ACT II

No cues

www.ingramcontent.com/pod-product-compliance
Ingram Content Group UK Ltd.
Pitfield, Milton Keynes, MK11 3LW, UK
UKHW021848210426
5322IPUK00022B/537